LOST LONDON

WYCH STREET, LOOKING EAST
FROM NEW INN GATEWAY

LOST LONDON

Being a description of *Landmarks*
which have disappeared *pictured* by
J. CROWTHER *circa* 1879-87 and
described by E. BERESFORD CHANCELLOR

"O! London won't be London long,
For 'twill be all pulled down;
And I shall sing a funeral song
O'er that time-honoured town."

Attributed to MAGINN.

PRINTED AT THE CHISWICK PRESS FOR
CONSTABLE AND COMPANY LIMITED
AND HOUGHTON MIFFLIN COMPANY
1926

PRINTED IN GREAT BRITAIN.

PREFACE

THE origin and scheme of the following book require a few words of explanation. The late Sir C. E. H. Chadwyck-Healey, K.C.B., K.C., employed an artist, J. Crowther, to make water-colour drawings of such features and landmarks throughout London as seemed likely to become before long a prey to the necessities for improvement and development. Crowther produced with indefatigable zeal a vast number of these, and as his skill as a topographical draughtsman was equalled by his artistic gifts, all these beautiful drawings are pictures in themselves apart from their great value as records of buildings which have disappeared within the last forty to fifty years.

When it was decided to publish a selection from them I was first asked to write descriptive accounts of each picture, but on consideration it was thought that a more or less continuous narrative concerning the places illustrated in the form of a peregrination (to use the old-fashioned word) from west to east and back again, would enable me to enlarge on each subject and also to touch on others germane to the matter. The actual arrangement of this itinerary was left to me, and I decided that the best course would be to begin at Chelsea and gradually to work along the north side of the river as far as the Strand, and then to cross the Thames by Waterloo Bridge (while one has the chance of doing so) and then wander for a time in the Borough before journeying on to Stockwell and so forth and returning to our starting point by way of Battersea Bridge.

The illustrations, for the most part, have been chosen with a special view to this arrangement; but two of them, which are outside the area covered, were included for reasons which appear in the text. These are Spa Fields Chapel and Royal Mint Street.

The name of Crowther is practically unknown, although a few of his water-colours were exhibited at various times at the Royal Academy. But his work has the authentic touch. His accuracy of detail; his keen sense of values; his unerring eye for topographical exposition, together with an artistic sense, not always present in such portrayals, combine in giving his work essential importance and value. The fact that he has recorded features which have long since disappeared and which other topographical draughtsmen have frequently overlooked, add so materially to this value and importance, that the selection here presented to the public can hardly fail to interest those who like to find recorded the lost features of London through the medium of artistic handiwork.

It is, indeed, because it is mainly the lost features of our city which are here illustrated and described that I call this book Lost London.

E. B. C.

CONTENTS

CHAPTER   PAGE

      PREFACE vii

      LIST OF ILLUSTRATIONS xi

  I. CHELSEA 1

 II. WESTMINSTER 14

III. SPRING GARDENS AND WHITEHALL 29

 IV. THE STRAND 42

  V. THE BOROUGH, SOUTHWARK 68

 VI. STOCKWELL, VAUXHALL, AND BATTERSEA . . 94

ix

LIST OF ILLUSTRATIONS

FACING
PAGE

WYCH STREET, LOOKING EAST FROM NEW INN GATEWAY

Frontispiece

1. MAUNDER'S FISH SHOP, NO. 72 CHEYNE WALK, CHELSEA . 2
2. TURNER'S HOUSE, NO. 119 CHEYNE WALK, CHELSEA . . 4
3. LAWRENCE STREET, CHELSEA—SOUTH-EAST CORNER . . 6
4. WHITELAND'S HOUSE, KING'S ROAD, CHELSEA . . 10
5. THE GREY COAT SCHOOL, WESTMINSTER . . . 14
6. EMERY HILL'S ALMSHOUSES, ROCHESTER ROW . . . 14
7. BUTLER'S ALMSHOUSES, WESTMINSTER . . . 16
8. LADY DACRE'S ALMSHOUSES—FRONT VIEW . . . 18
9. LADY DACRE'S ALMSHOUSES—GARDEN FRONT . . . 20
10. LADY DACRE'S ALMSHOUSES—THE CHAPEL . . . 22
11. OLD HOUSES IN PYE STREET, WESTMINSTER . . . 24
12. OLD ARCHWAY TENEMENT, BROADWAY, WESTMINSTER . . 26
13. OLD HOUSE AT THE CORNER OF TOTHILL STREET AND BROAD-
WAY 26
14. JUDGE JEFFREYS' HOUSE, DELAHAY STREET, WESTMINSTER . 28
15. SPRING GARDENS FROM THE MALL 30
16. PASSAGE IN SPRING GARDENS FROM TRAFALGAR SQUARE TO
THE MALL 32
17. ST. MATTHEW'S CHAPEL, SPRING GARDENS . . . 34
18. THE GUN HOUSE, SPRING GARDENS 36
19. THE ALMONRY OFFICE, WHITEHALL 38
20. WHITEHALL YARD, VANBRUGH'S HOUSE IN THE BACKGROUND 40
21. OLD HOUSES IN THE STRAND, NEXT TO THE ADELPHI THEATRE 42
22. OLD HOUSES IN THE STRAND, EAST END OF ST. MARY'S
CHURCH 44

FACING
PAGE

23. GOLDEN BUILDINGS, STRAND 46
24. STRAND LANE, LOOKING NORTH 48
25. STRAND LANE, LOOKING TOWARDS THE RIVER . . . 48
26. SIR WILLIAM CONGREVE'S HOUSE, SOUTH END OF CECIL
   STREET, STRAND 50
27. IVY BRIDGE LANE, STRAND, LOOKING SOUTH . . . 52
28. EXCHANGE COURT, STRAND 54
29. LORD DYSART'S HOUSE AT THE CORNER OF NORFOLK STREET 56
30. THE CHESHIRE CHEESE, OLD SQUARE, SURREY STREET . . 58
31. THE ARUNDEL HOTEL, ARUNDEL STREET—EMBANKMENT
   FRONT 60
32. THE STRAND, OPPOSITE THE LAW COURTS . . . 60
33. EAST END OF HOLYWELL STREET AND WYCH STREET . 64
34. HOLYWELL STREET, LOOKING WEST 66
35. WATERLOO BRIDGE FROM CHARING CROSS RAILWAY BRIDGE 68
36. OLD WOODEN HOUSES IN ROYAL MINT STREET . . . 68
37. THE WHITE HART INN, BOROUGH 70
38. YARD OF THE GEORGE INN, BOROUGH . . . 72
39. THE KING'S HEAD INN, BOROUGH 72
40. THE YARD OF THE QUEEN'S HEAD INN, BOROUGH . . 74
41. BACK VIEW OF THE QUEEN'S HEAD INN, BOROUGH . . 76
42. INTERIOR OF THE WHITE LYON PRISON . . . 78
43. MARSHALSEA PRISON—A SKY-PARLOUR 80
44. MARSHALSEA PLACE—PORTION OF THE DEBTORS PRISON . 82
45. ANGEL COURT, WITH PORTION OF THE MARSHALSEA PRISON
   WALL 84
46. QUEEN'S BENCH PRISON—THE CANTEEN 86
47. QUEEN'S BENCH PRISON—THE CHAPEL 88
48. QUEEN'S BENCH PRISON—THE PRISONERS' YARD . . 88
49. OLD HOUSES IN SNOWFIELDS, BERMONDSEY . . . 90
50. ANCIENT TENEMENTS IN BERMONDSEY STREET . . . 92

LIST OF ILLUSTRATIONS

FACING
PAGE

51. THE SURREY CHAPEL, BLACKFRIARS ROAD 94
52. SPA FIELDS CHAPEL   98
53. HOUSES ON WEST SIDE OF CHURCH STREET, LAMBETH   . 100
54. TURRET HOUSE, SOUTH LAMBETH   102
55. CARRON OR CARON HOUSE, VAUXHALL   106
56. STOCKWELL PARK HOUSE, FROM STOCKWELL PARK   .   . 110
57. STOCKWELL PARK HOUSE—GARDEN FRONT   .   .   . 112
58. THE RAVEN INN, BATTERSEA   114
59. OLD BATTERSEA BRIDGE, FROM THE NORTH BANK   .   . 116

LOST LONDON

CHAPTER I

CHELSEA

IF we were to compare the divisions of London with the members of
a family Chelsea should, I think, be regarded as the unconventional
scion of a stock that was otherwise conventional enough—the
artistic offspring, as it were, concerning whom the rest were never
quite certain; the breakaway about whose doings there was something
of an erratic air. For Chelsea has always been to London in the nature
of an enigma. It is in it but never quite of it; and there still pervades
it an atmosphere of antiquity strangely blending with that artistic *aura*
which has now become its specialized possession. Its name conjures
up not so much the personalities of the great historic figures who once
wandered about it—More and Erasmus, Swift and Sloane, and the
rest—as those of the artists who have worked here and have dwelt lovingly
on its incomparable river reaches where the sun goes down in the mist
among the campanili of commerce and the warehouses which the mystic
twilight evokes into lordly palaces. It is of Rossetti (who, curiously,
cared for none of these things) and Turner and Whistler (to whom they
meant so much) and Sargent's amazing achievement and Mr. Augustus
John's dominating brush that we think when we mention Chelsea, even
to the exclusion of the philosopher who sits wearily brooding, in Boehm's
bronze, over his present which is now our past, and pessimistically
speculating on a future which owed its chief horror to the very last
source he would have been inclined to suggest.

As we pass along the Cheyne Walk of to-day not even much
rebuilding, and the destruction of much which memory holds dear, can
obliterate the past, and one visualizes a ghostly Dick Steele coming out

of an unsubstantial Don Saltero's, or Sir Hans Sloane solemnly passing into the Manor House to greet there older ghosts than his: Lord Hamilton and Lord Howard of Effingham, Anne of Cleves and the Duchess of Northumberland, the Lord High Admiral Seymour, and Lady Jane Grey and Catherine Parr, and the burly straddling figure of the Defender of the Faith himself. Monsieur St. Evrémond (with that monstrous wart between his eyes) and the once beautiful and still attractive lady who queened it at the Merry Monarch's court flit about the site of Paradise Row, now, alas! with them in the past; and innumerable other figures less outstanding, but once essentially part of the little village, are to be met in their spiritual guise: Messenger Monsey and Mr. Cheyne, Cruden and Mary Astell and Mr. Nield, Dominicetti, known by his baths, and Constantine Jennings, remembered by his dog.

But these are but ghosts, and it is Rossetti and his circle, and Whistler and his, and the Queen's House and Lindsay House and the White House where they foregathered, that seem actual realities—where the artistic ghosts have as corporeal a being as have happily the architectural settings in which they moved. Chelsea is, in a word, to London what Art is to Life; by some admired; wondered at by many; by more visualized with a slight feeling of uncertainty, almost of distrust.

It is, I think, suggestive that Crowther, instead of reproducing pictures of those more architecturally important buildings such as the old church, Lindsay House, or the dignified residences in Cheyne Walk, which he no doubt felt would be likely to be preserved and were not so much in need of pictorial perpetuation, chose rather as the *motif* of one of his exquisite water-colour sketches a little old-world shop which experience told him would be a probable prey to the " improver."

The exiguous shop, the picturesque features of which he has thus reproduced, stood in that part of Cheyne Walk once known as Lombard Street, into which Danvers Street runs, where stood some of Chelsea's oldest houses, among them the mansion of John de Shordich, which dated from the fourteenth century, the Dog Inn, also of great antiquity, and the Bell, at the corner of Danvers Street, opposite the once well-known Chelsea Ferry commemorated by Dibdin in one of his songs. The little fish shop, kept by Mrs. Elizabeth Maunder, which

MAUNDER'S FISH SHOP, NO. 72 CHEYNE WALK, CHELSEA

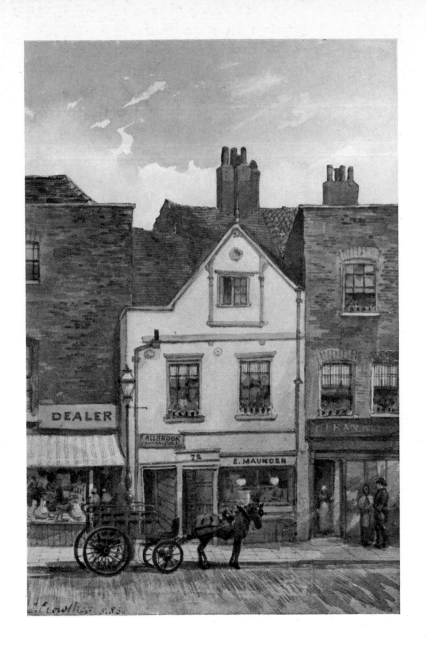

forms the chief feature of Crowther's picture, stood four doors to the west of the Rising Sun, the successor to the Dog Tavern referred to. The plain plaster front of the little house was relieved by the woodwork of the gable and that forming a kind of frame to the upper window. Above this window the small circle indicates a terra-cotta medallion with a head in relief, which, when the house was demolished, was happily preserved and is now in the Chelsea Library. The shop portion of the building is famous through Whistler's well-known etching dated 1890, and it is a curious fact that the house in which he died, in 1903, was built on the site of this very structure which was pulled down in 1892. Mr. C. R. Ashbee, the well-known antiquary, erected the house, which is numbered 74 Cheyne Walk, and is noticeable on account of its original exterior and its door of beaten copper.

In a city which is rapidly losing so many of its essential qualities of picturesqueness, where great buildings are taking the place of lesser architectural features, Chelsea is one of the few places in which something of the old charm still resides; something of the atmosphere of a more restful period lingers still. The very names of its streets and byways conjure up a period that seems already eons away: Danvers Street, Lawrence Street, Cheyne Walk, and Glebe Place have an almost Augustan air about them, and not yet do the spirits of Mr. Spectator or Sir Roger de Coverley seem wholly to have deserted their calm and rather shy recesses.

Indeed, in Cheyne Walk we can recapture the atmosphere of the eighteenth century more thoroughly perhaps than in any other spot in London. For even the Mall, with all its old-world memories, has become somewhat sophisticated under a new and hardly yet accustomed guise. There we do but vaguely visualize the crowd that once passed up and down beneath its formal trees and took their pleasure around its formal ponds. The brocades and lute-strings, the flowered waistcoats and the glittering swords, the play of fan and snuff-box there seem to elude us; and who can think of sedan chairs with the constant whirr of the headlong motor in their ears? Even the presence of the red-brick royal residence is hardly sufficient to recall the mind to the days before Buckingham House had been stuccoed into Buckingham Palace; before Stafford House and Clarence House had arisen on the sites of less imposing but

3

TURNER'S HOUSE

No. 119 CHEYNE WALK, CHELSEA

As one looks at that tiny coign of vantage one can visualize the old man getting up every morning at daybreak and clambering up to the balcony on the roof " with blanket or dressing-gown carelessly thrown over him . . . to see the sun rise and to observe the colour flow flashing back into the pale morning sky," as Thornbury describes him. Till his last illness he did this, and even within an hour of his death " his landlady wheeled his chair to the window to enable him to look upon the sun-shine mantling the river and illuminating the sails of the passing boats." " The window of his death chamber," adds Ruskin, " was turned towards the West, and the sun shone upon his face in its setting and rested there as he expired."

Crowther's drawing shows us the tiny cottage substantially as it was in Turner's time. To-day changes have occurred here. Together with the similar dwelling next door it has been converted into a single house, and something of a modern air has been imparted to it. But after all, its walls, although denuded of their ivy, are the walls that once Turner knew; the windows are those from which he gazed; the iron balustrade that on which, like some denizen of the East, he worshipped the sun in its rising and setting; and if the erection of the hideous block of build-ings on the west has largely stultified the advantages of the little balcony, at least the sun rises and sets through the grey mists of the river of history, and those who relish it can never forget the memory of the man who watched it for the last time these some and seventy years ago.[1]

It is but a little way from this hallowed spot to Lawrence Street, but one can hardly pass Chelsea's old church without stopping a moment to admire its warm brickwork and exquisite setting. It is one of the few remaining buildings of the kind that were once common enough in the environs of London; to-day you may seek long for its equal in charm of colouring and outline. The first specific mention of a church at this spot occurs in the year 1291, although it is probable that a Saxon place of worship originally stood here. Of the existing building, the chancel and the Lawrence Chapel are the oldest portions, and they date from the

---

[1] Bryan, writing in 1869, says " the roadway in front of Turner's little house has been considerably widened . . . a *handsome* terrace has been erected besides a number of houses on the adjoining ground."

fourteenth century. In 1528 Sir Thomas More is supposed to have erected the chapel, which still bears his name; certainly some of its carvings are obviously traceable to the Italian artificers who came over to England during that period; indeed, it has been conjectured that Holbein, a friend of More, may have been responsible for certain portions of the design.

It is pleasant to think of More and his family coming from the manor house near by to worship in Chelsea Church; and when we look round his chapel we see much that he saw; as well as the spot where his body rests beneath the monument on the south wall, on which appears the long Latin inscription he himself composed, with a gap in the lettering where the word " heretics " is said once to have been. But many other notable people are also buried here, and the Lawrence Chapel contains not only the tomb of various members of that once well-known Chelsea family, but of Sir Robert Stanley, son of the sixth Earl of Derby, the opening line of whose epitaph, " To say a Stanley lies here, that alone were epitaph enough," strikes at once a splendid and complacent note of praise. Here, too, is the altar-tomb to Lady Jane Guildford, Duchess of Northumberland, the mother of the ill-fated Lord Guildford Dudley and of the luckier Earl of Leicester of Queen Elizabeth's predilection. And we have special reason to observe the tomb of Anne, Lady Dacre, not only because of its beauty but because we shall come later to those almshouses in Westminster of which she was the munificent patron.

Outside the church the monuments, though of a later date, are hardly less interesting: here are commemorated that Dr. Chamberlayne who wrote *The Present State of England*, a book of reference which many have found valuable; Phillip Miller, once curator of the neighbouring Physic Garden, and, although a forgotten worthy, called in his day "The Prince of Gardeners "; Woodfall, whose name is preserved as that of the printer of the *Letters of Junius*; and Sir Hans Sloane, whose serpent-entwined urn has for so many years been a landmark at this spot, just as his statue, by Rysbrack, has been in the Physic Garden where it so appropriately stands. It is hard to leave Chelsea Church with so many other points of interest about it calling for recognition; and one cannot do so without at least noting that in 1667 the old tower and much of the

6

LAWRENCE STREET, CHELSEA

South-east Corner

west portion of the building were demolished in order that a larger structure might be erected. In five years from that date this rebuilding was completed, and the church emerged much as we know it to-day, although, of course, since then many alterations and repairs have been from time to time necessary.

And at last we reach the Lawrence Street of Crowther's delightful water-colour drawing. Its name perpetuates, of course, the residence here of that Lawrence family, members of which, as we have seen, lie buried in the old church, to whom the Manor was granted by Henry VIII. It is one of the oldest of existing Chelsea thoroughfares, although to-day there are but fragments in it to remind us of past times. Crowther, who made his drawing in 1882, was able, however, to preserve some of those elements of picturesqueness which have in the intervening forty odd years disappeared, as those having his picture in their mind's eyes will realize if they wander up and down the street to-day. Nearly forty years before he sketched it, one of its chief features was being demolished. At its north end stood Lawrence House, where Sir Reginald Bray, who had fought on Henry VII's side at Bosworth and was for so much in the building of that king's chapel at Westminster as well as of St. George's Chapel at Windsor (where he is buried, by the way); and Sir William (afterwards Lord) Sandys; and the Lawrences; and after them Monmouth's widowed duchess (when it was re-named Monmouth House) had all lived. But in spite of this illustrious roll the most notable occupant of Monmouth House was Dr. Tobias Smollett, writing feverishly, continually over-spending his income, hospitably entertaining here such as Johnson and Goldsmith and Sterne, Garrick and Wilkes and John Hunter, and showing himself the kind and liberal friend to less notable and successful men. When Carlyle came to Chelsea in 1834, he speaks of Monmouth House as being then in a process of demolition; so that when Crowther perpetuated what of picturesqueness there remained in Lawrence Street, its most notable feature was but a memory. To-day there are a few nice old houses on the west side at the north end of the street; and an elaborate over-doorway opposite suggests that the building now divided, to which it gives a double access, was once a single and imposing residence. But at the river end new erections

7

have obliterated the old-world air which clings desperately to the portion which has not yet been *improved*.

It is the appearance of this river end of Lawrence Street that is preserved for us in this beautiful little picture. That these picturesque structures should have disappeared in favour of the Hospital for Sick Children [1] should console us for their loss, a consolation we should have difficulty in experiencing had a huge block of flats replaced them. But apart from the excellent work it does, the architecture of the Hospital is such a painful exhibition of the decorative exertions of a bad period that one almost wishes its foundation, instead of being in 1875, had been delayed for half a century. It is an interesting fact that it was in one of the demolished houses, round the corner and facing the river, that Holman Hunt painted his "Light of the World"; the presence here, then, of a hospital devoted to the welfare of little children is specially appropriate.

One can reach the King's Road from Cheyne Walk by all sorts of ways, hardly one of which will fail to reveal some interesting landmark or the site of the abode of some outstanding figure. Few, if any, parts of London are indeed so instinct with such memories as Chelsea, and if the reader is like me, nothing pleases him more than to wander about its purlieus and to try and recapture the atmosphere which lingers in its curious little byways and has not wholly been driven away by the incursion of the beautiful modern houses on the Embankment or the presence elsewhere of more utilitarian structures.

For instance, you may begin by way of Church Street, and in order to avoid much that jars in what was once called by a famous Chelsea resident " one of the most interesting streets in the whole world," may cut through little Justice Walk (what a delightful name!), at the corner of which once stood the famous Chelsea china factory (established in 1745), if factory be not too prosaic a term for what rather resembles the airiness of sea-foam or the iridescence of the sunbeam. Soon we shall reach Upper Cheyne Row, where a writer lived whose works have so often a similar lightness and fantastical grace, although he could be severe in his

---

[1] It should not be forgotten that this benefaction was due to the generosity of Mr. and Mrs. Wickham Flower.

satire on occasion, and once went to prison for some too outspoken comments on the first Gentleman of Europe. For it was in Upper Cheyne Walk that Leigh Hunt lived; and you may still see his abode, not much altered, outwardly at any rate, since the time when, in 1834, Carlyle was his neighbour, and described his household as " nondescript! unutterable!—a poetical Tinkerdom, without parallel even in literature." And so by the long, unlovely Oakley Street into the rush and turmoil of the main thoroughfare which is, after all, one of London's most picturesque streets, with its old houses desperately clinging here and there to a frail existence; its tree-lined pavements; its *aura* of the arts—a kind of suburban Montmartre.

Or better, perhaps, as we want to reach the east end of the King's Road, will it be to keep along the river-front; so altered by its embankment; so changed in many architectural features, but still fascinating from its memories and the red-brick which has survived so many and drastic changes. For every house here seems instinct with history and contains, one feels sure, many an illustrious ghost. Here Henry VIII had a manor house (or so it was called), and at least sent his little daughter Elizabeth to live in the salubrious air when she was but three or four years old. Hither, too, in 1543 came Catherine of Aragon, and another of the much-married monarch's wives was destined to die here fourteen years later—the amiable, compliant Anne of Cleves. The history of this great house with its innumerable famous occupants would delay us overmuch were we to loiter even about the outskirts of its annals. And, after all, for there is nothing to point where the fabric stood, we are but leaving memories, as we pass along Paradise Row, where once and till so relatively recently, that famous little collocation of seventeenth-century houses stood, one of the most representative bits of old Chelsea, where the Duchess of Mazarin and St. Evrémond lived and my Lady Castlewood, and where, no doubt, Mr. Henry Esmond himself visited.

And so along the whole façade of Wren's Hospital, and up Franklin's Row (so much more charming a name than the Burton Court into which it has been metamorphosed), so called after the Mr. Franklin who, in 1693, presented some brass chandeliers to the old church, and we come to Cheltenham Terrace, which brings us out into the King's Road at the

9

spot where Crowther's lamp-post stands in such marked antithesis to the Whitelands House of our search, with its dear little overhanging window and beautiful iron gateway asserting its origin in spite of the stucco and prim formality of a later period.

There it stands as it stood till 1890; and but for the artist's instinct to preserve pictorially what was picturesque (and thus seemingly doomed) we might have difficulty in recalling what so many of us could so easily remember. Unfortunately there is little to be gathered concerning its history, and the combined investigations of such special Chelsea historians as Faulkner, Bryan, Beaver, and Blunt have not succeeded in tracing the name of its builder or indeed very much concerning its annals. It is, however, known to have been in existence in 1772, for in that year a discourse on "Female Education and Christian Fortitude under Affliction" was delivered here by the Rev. John Jenkins, at which time the premises were occupied by a young ladies' school. Indeed, its scholastic traditions survived into the nineteenth century, for down to 1842 it was being carried on by the Misses Babington for a like purpose.

In that year the house was taken by the National Society on a long lease; and in 1850 a meeting was held in London for the purpose of raising funds for the erection of the "college" which, soon after, came into existence. Bryan, writing in 1869, says: "The Institution provides for the education, maintenance, and training of more than 100 young women, between the ages of 18 and 25, who purpose to become teachers of National schools; and secondly, for the daily instruction of children of the neighbourhood, in four schools."

When Whitelands College was erected, the old house remained as we see it in Crowther's picture, probably as the residence of the Principal, but in 1890 it was demolished, and in the following year was replaced by buildings more nearly approximating, from an architectural point of view, with the College itself. The old beaten iron gateway, with its lamp-extinguishers, was, however, preserved and erected at the entrance to the new structure. Beaver, in his history of Chelsea, gives a little picture which he himself drew of the old house as it appeared in 1890.

It is not necessary here to say anything about the annals and work

WHITELAND'S HOUSE, KING'S ROAD, CHELSEA

C

WHITELAND'S HOUSE, KING'S ROAD, CHELSEA

of Whitelands College, but I may remind the reader that it was identified with those May Day festivities inaugurated in 1881 by Ruskin, references to which will be found in *Praeterita* and others of his works. The college buildings can hardly be regarded as architectural ornaments to the King's Road, but they were erected at a bad period, and at least for many years the picturesqueness of old Whitelands House formed a purple patch on their otherwise purely utilitarian outlines.

It is pleasant to return to the tree-lined Embankment, but as we skirt the river from Chelsea to Westminster we shall find that remarkable changes have occurred within the last fifty years. In the first place the Embankment was not formed till about 1876, and before its advent an irregular brick wall, here and there intercepted by steps and landing stages, divided the roadway from the Thames. Since those days gardens have been laid out here; new houses have been erected; and something of an urban air has come to dominate the spot. But much, happily, remains (although to be sure the exquisite Paradise Row has disappeared) capable of carrying one's mind back to less sophisticated times. Many beautiful structures with their iron gateways are still there; and as one passes along Cheyne Walk one can hardly point to a single residence without being able to connect with it some famous name. There lived Rossetti, in the house which Richard Chapman had built in 1717,[1] with his menagerie and his eggs and bacon, and Swinburne dreaming in his corner; there, for a time, sojourned George Eliot; and Mrs. Gaskell a little further west. William Bell Scott's one time home, and those of the more peripatetic Whistler, recall Victorian days; but the worn red-brick work links that age with earlier ones, and it is the spirit of the Georgian era and that of Anne and even of Caroline days that remains here in spite of Crosby Hall in its alien environment, and in spite of rebuilding and demolition, forming a link between the Tudor atmosphere, now only existing in the fabric of the church and in tradition, and our own period.

[1] This is No. 16 Cheyne Walk, and has frequently been associated with Catherine of Braganza, because it was known as the Queen's House. As, however, none of the residences from No. 1 to No. 40 was built before Sir Hans Sloane began to lay out his property here in 1712, and as Catherine left England finally in 1692, this attribution is obviously incorrect.

The actual river reach has been stultified by those suspension bridges, one of which took the place of old Battersea Bridge which, closed to vehicular traffic in 1883, was pulled down four years later after something over a century's picturesque life. But it is still the river—"the liquid history" of Mr. John Burns's felicitous phrase—that forms the inalienable foreground of romance that still haunts all this part of what was once an outlying suburb but is now an integral part of London. Behind the trees of its embankment rise the red bricks of old days and the red bricks of modernism. But the latter cannot quite dominate the past here as they have done in other parts of the city, because the insistent river flows still as it flowed then; because the Queen's House and Chelsea Hospital are still landmarks which, in spite of iron railings and macadamized roads, hold their own; because, by the grace of God, that most awful exposition of the necessities of urban life, the tramway, has not come to desecrate this yet pleasant spot; has not touched its essential distinction with the vulgarism of overhead wires nor introduced the hateful uniformity of outline and mode of progression of such things into these recessed parts of the metropolis; with the result that from Chelsea old church to Chelsea Bridge Road the thoroughfare remains one of the few in which one can walk with ease and safety.

As we pass along what the eighteenth century would have called this "umbrageous road," we can peep into the Physic Garden where its deity, Sir Hans Sloane, stands in Rysbrack's stone, and can dream, further along, of the Ranelagh which once reigned by the side of Wren's great hospital—the Ranelagh which focussed in itself the sophisticated *aura* of the most decorative of centuries. Do the Chelsea Pensioners, one wonders, ever see through their dim eyes the ghosts of all that gallant company parading the sites where the Rotunda and the bosky arbours once stood? Do they hear at the witching hour the nightingales silenced by Mrs. Storer or Miss Formantel, or the tinkling, tremulous notes of the harpsichord swallowed up by the choruses of "Acis and Galatea," or the blare of Bonnell Thornton's "Burlesque Ode"? But the mighty river has heard these sounds, and here, where it begins one of its graceful curves (and it is these curves that make it so much more effective a waterway, as it is so much ampler than the

Seine at Paris) we come into Grosvenor Road, and Grosvenor Road is an object lesson in how we have wilfully disregarded the opportunities which the river has given us. Instead of a continued embankment we are driven inland by wharves and yards (just as yards and wharves and disgraceful warehouses are still permitted to spoil the south bank), and we may profitably hurry our steps past these buildings and others as squalid until we reach the Tate Gallery, whose classic outlines on the spot where the pepper pots of Millbank Penitentiary once gave a sort of quasi-mediaeval air to this neighbourhood, is flanked by the red brick of the Royal Army Medical College on the one hand and the Military Hospital on the other.

CHAPTER II

WESTMINSTER

IT is at this point that we can leave the river by Horseferry Road, interesting for nothing but the fact that it perpetuates by its name the existence of that ferry across the Thames (the only one permitted in London) by which the fugitive James fled on the night of 10th December 1688, and, incidentally, dropped the great seal in the water as he was being rowed across.

We here enter a neighbourhood which has in recent years undergone drastic changes, and yet much of which still retains that old-world air that gives to its exiguous streets and byways around the Abbey the cloistral atmosphere of a cathedral city. And even much of the new building hereabouts does not detract from this; for there has, happily, been a consensus of appreciation of the appropriateness of the Georgian convention, not only in the domestic architecture but also in official and commercial erections here; and those who regret the disappearance of many old houses in Smith Square and its purlieus may be to some extent consoled by the erection in their place of work embodying the same tradition and shedding around something of the same warmth of colouring. And certain landmarks remain: Archer's fantastic church is one of them, with its four towers, of which such different people as Lord Chesterfield and Charles Dickens made fun, and its air of settling down into the marshy ground in which its inadequate foundations were laid; while in Grey Coat Street stands another, the Grey Coat Hospital, which was founded in 1698 for the education and maintenance of seventy boys and forty girls of the poorer classes in St. Margaret's parish. By a subsequent foundation some nine years later, the parish of St. John the Evangelist was included; the number of those benefited having already been increased in 1701. Just thirteen years before Crowther made his drawing of the place, it had been changed into a day-school for little

14

THE GREY COAT SCHOOL, WESTMINSTER

THE GREY COAT SCHOOL, WESTMINSTER

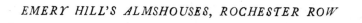

EMERY HILL'S ALMSHOUSES, ROCHESTER ROW

girls who wear their grey cloaks " with a difference " from what their predecessors did in the seventeenth and eighteenth centuries.

The accompanying picture may be illustrated by what Walcott, in his *Memorials of Westminster*, had to say about the structure in 1849. " This hospital," he writes, " presents a considerable line of frontage towards Grey-Coat-Place, from which it is separated by a large court-yard. It is composed of a central building, ornamented with a clock, turret, and bell above the Royal Arms of Queen Anne, with the motto, 'Semper eadem' flanked by a figure on either side dressed in the former costume of the children. The south side, which looks out upon an open garden and spacious detached playgrounds (the whole surrounded by an extensive wall), contains the school-rooms. Above is a wainscoted dining-hall, used for the private prayers of the Hospital. The dormi-tories occupy the whole attic storey. The board-room, highly panelled, a very handsome apartment, contains full-length portraits of the royal foundress Queen Anne." To-day changes have taken place; and although the actual building remains as it was in 1886 when Crowther sketched it, the presence of ugly warehouses opposite, if it accentuates the old-world beauty of the Hospital, has brought into its purlieus a note of modernism—a discordant note.

In this picture we happily only see the pretty old structure itself with its forecourt hidden, but for an iron gateway, from the road by the wall on the right, a wall which, for obvious reasons, has had to be surmounted, as we see, by an iron trellis. As you go from St. Peter Street into Rochester Row, you might well pass by without observing this beautiful relic of an earlier day. Its entrance, through which its façade can be glimpsed, is opposite the station of the Fire Brigade, whose assistance one devoutly hopes may never have to be invoked on its behalf.

Close by, in Rochester Row, were some almshouses instituted in 1708 by one Emery Hill, whose name they bear. They were founded for the accommodation of six poor men and their wives as well as for six widows, and there was a boys' school attached to them. Crowther has perpetuated their outlines in the picture (here reproduced) which he made of the collocation of little brick cottages in 1880.

To-day this benefaction has become incorporated with those of

15

This area was at one time a great place for almshouses and charitable schools. The Blue Coat School, at the east end of James Street, was founded in 1688, and the picturesque building, happily still remaining, was erected in 1709. It can be reached through that curious little byway, Horse Shoe Alley, and at the back abuts on the tiny green oasis known as Brewer's Green. In the year of its erection a Mr. William Green built a school and a master's house adjoining it in Little Chapel Street, in which were some almshouses, as there were in York Street; while the Green Coat School, in Dacre Street, was founded in 1633 and rebuilt in 1700, Dr. Busby being a liberal benefactor. This was merged in the United Westminster Schools in 1873-8.

Concerning Lady Dacre's Almshouses and their adjoining chapel, alternatively called Emmanuel Hospital, data is fuller. We have already met with the tomb of the pious foundress of this institution in Chelsea Church, where she lies beneath an imposing monument. She was an outstanding resident in Chelsea, and was one of the many illustrious people who once occupied the old house of Sir Thomas More, which had been granted by Henry VIII to Sir William Paulet, afterwards first Marquess of Winchester. Lady Dacre was daughter of the Marchioness of Winchester by her first husband, Sir Richard Sackville, and therefore sister of Thomas Sackville, who became Earl of Dorset, and wrote *Gorbuduc*, the earliest of English tragedies. She married Gregory, Lord Dacre, by whom the famous house was bequeathed to Lord Burleigh, who is supposed to have reconstructed it before selling it to the Earl of Lincoln. But it is with Lady Dacre and her charitable endowment rather than with her one time residence that we are here concerned; and we find that it was by her will, dated 20th December 1594, that she founded the "Hospital of Jesus," as it was first called, a foundation confirmed by charter in 1601. It provided for the maintenance of twenty-four old men and women, sixteen of whom were to be parishioners of St. Margaret's. The Dacres once possessed a residence called Stourton House, at the entrance of old Tothill Street, a house mentioned by Stow and still existing into the second half of the last century in Dacre Street, leading out of Broadway (where some old dilapidated houses have but recently been demolished), and having grounds which occupied the site of what was afterwards known as Strutton (a corruption of Stourton) Ground, into whose booth-lined fastnesses a cinema has penetrated! Lady Dacre had, therefore, a personal interest in this locality, and hence its selection as the site of her benefaction.

The original Hospital, known by the name of Emmanuel as well as Lady Dacre's, was actually erected in 1600, but becoming ruinous in the reign of Queen Anne, was then rebuilt, the adjoining chapel being erected in the time of George II, and the schoolrooms in our own day. The Endowed Schools Commission of 1873 began its work of reform in this foundation; and, in consequence, vast changes have taken place in the internal economy of the place since the far-off days of its institution.[1] Among the masters of the Hospital was the Rev. William Beloe, who translated *Herodotus* and wrote a well-known gossiping book called *The Sexagenarian*. He occupied the post from 1783 to 1808; while a certain poor inmate was a Mrs. Windymore, a cousin of Queen Mary II and Queen Anne, who, according to Walcott, died in one of these lowly dwellings in 1772, within a stone's throw of the spot where her two royal relations had been crowned queens of England!

Of the three pictures we have here of Lady Dacre's Hospital the first (*vide Plate*) is perhaps the most interesting, as it shows a considerable portion of the warm red-bricked structure and particularly the elaborate iron gateway and railings which were once such a feature at this spot. The almshouses, with their chapel, stood just east of the little Blue Coat School,[2] which, in spite of Besant's prognostications, still happily survives, at the spot where James Street joins what is now Caxton Street, but was formerly known as Chapel Street. The Blue Coat School is just outside the picture, on the left. The large block of modern erections in the background are those formerly known as Peabody Buildings, but now as Chandos House.

Crowther's second drawing (*vide Plate*), here reproduced in colour, shows us the garden of the almshouses and the chapel, with its

[1] Emmanuel Hospital was pulled down in January 1894, after having been empty for some months.

[2] This school was founded in 1688, the present building, so reminiscent of Wren, being erected in 1709.

18

LADY DACRE'S ALMSHOUSES

Front View

D

LADY DACRE'S ALMS HOUSES

Front View

heavily ornamented pediment and clock and bell turret above. A modern touch is given to the picture by the presence of the lamp-post, but otherwise the whole place seems to breathe of ancient peace, and to have been one in which we might expect to see the figures of Frederick Walker slowly pacing out their time and hanging superfluous on the stage of life.

The third water-colour (*vide Plate*) represents the interior of the chapel and speaks for itself. Its architectural features are characteristically eighteenth century, as are the curious and apparently extremely uncomfortable pews. But a link with an earlier day is communicated to it by the presence in the background of a beautiful late sixteenth-century tomb which I imagine to have been that of Lord Dacre (a man's recumbent figure is discernible on it), whose widow showed herself so great a benefactor to Westminster. The stone, near the lectern, and the ugly gas-bracket indicate, on the other hand, the inartistic utilitarianism of our own earlier day.

The formation of Victoria Street which, projected in 1844, was first opened to the public in 1851, greatly changed the appearance of much of this part of Westminster, for if it actually only cut through certain old streets and demolished old houses in its direct line, its coming was responsible for drastic alterations in the alignment of neighbouring thoroughfares and byways; and, with the enlargement of Broad Sanctuary and the formation of Parliament Square (on the site of which blocks of houses formerly stood, as may be seen in Capon's drawings[1]), may be said to have put the finishing touch to the reconstruction of this part inaugurated by the building of the new Houses of Parliament.

Among certain ancient thoroughfares, however, which were unaffected by these developments was Old Pye Street, and Old Pye Street is one of those sites which Crowther selected as *motifs* for his skilful handling. It links up St. Anne's Street with the Strutton Ground, to which I have already referred, a part of which at one time was known as Duck Lane. It derived its name from that Sir Robert Pye, John Hampden's son-in-law, who once lived in it, and who, together with Isaac de

---

[1] Published by the London Topographical Society; others are in the Westminster Public Library.

was made in 1883, and by it we can see at a glance what changes have been wrought here during the intervening period between then and now.

At one time, well within the memory of many of us, a variety of old structures which had outlived their period and had become ruinous and rat-riddled and, therefore, not unpicturesque, could be seen in this quarter. Until quite recently a few were to be found in Petty France, although that monstrosity, Queen Anne's Mansions (fancy anyone being daring enough to couple that Queen's name with which we associate such urbanity in architectural expression with this negation of taste and decency!), and the red-brick building which was once associated with panoramas and then wonderingly blossomed forth as "Niagara," stultified any attempts to keep this little corner beautiful. Nearly all these old "bits" have now gone, and if remembering happier things is the bitterest part of sorrow (as we have classic authority for believing), then those are happy who do not remember this part of Westminster in its pristine condition.

Crowther has at least rescued the memory of one of these survivals in the quaint little domicile, like a domestic bridge of sighs, which once stood in Broadway. I seem to remember it, but cannot be quite certain. If, however, I am not mistaken I think it gave entrance to what was known as King's Head Cottages, nearly opposite the St. James's Park Station on the north side of the street. There used certainly to be a tailor's there, and by the drawing we see the word "clothier" on the upper part of the house on the left-hand side of the entrance to what appears to be a *cul-de-sac* (as King's Head Cottages was), rather than a passage-way to another thoroughfare. As an alternative this particular little plaster-covered dwelling (no doubt dating from the seventeenth century) may have been either on the east or west side of that portion of Broadway which runs towards Victoria Street, as in Horwood's plan there are shown several *impasses* there. The point is not, perhaps, of great moment; the chief interest in the picture being its commemoration of a quaint relic of an earlier day, which succeeded in surviving till the 'eighties of the last century.

According to William Stow, who published his *Remarks* on London in 1722 and is not, of course, to be confounded with his great topographical

21

forerunner, John Stow, there used formerly to be a market for hay held here, which, however, he speaks of as being discontinued in his day. He also refers to the White Horse and Black Horse inns as being situated close by, and there is little doubt that the White Horse Street I have already mentioned took its name from the former. Dick Turpin is traditionally associated with these inns (he actually lived in one of the numerous small courts off Broadway), and is said to have set off thence on many of his depredatory expeditions; but that the Black Horse Inn took its name from his famous steed, as asserted by Walcott, is clearly inaccurate, as the highwayman was only about eleven years of age in 1722 when Stow speaks of the place as then bearing that name.

The name of Tothill, Tuthill, or Tuttle, as it is variously spelt, is one of great antiquity. We know it to-day as that of the street which was formerly practically the main thoroughfare from the Abbey purlieus to the west; but so far back as the reign of Henry III it designated generally the manor, which embraced a large portion of the ground hereabouts, and which then appertained to John Maunsel, Lord High Chancellor of England, Tothill Fields, spreading away to the south of the district around Vincent Square and so forth. The history of this large tract of ground does not immediately concern us here, although it may be noted that this area, in common with others in London now thickly covered by houses, was at one time a selected spot for tournaments and for those open-air distractions in which the citizen of former times delighted; while wagers of battle were here settled and their equivalents at a later period, viz., duels, took place and were, indeed, common enough. The gardens of Tothill Fields were noted in the seventeenth century, and Howell, the author of *Londinopolis* (although not in that work, but in a letter to a friend), speaks of melons being raised here. There was also a Maze in the Fields, referred to by Aubrey and shown in one of Hollar's plans, while the place was selected as one of those where the dead during the Plague were buried—much to the distress of Pepys, who was " troubled " when he heard of it.

Tothill Street, with which we *are* concerned, is one of very ancient origin, and Stow mentions it as, in his time, containing various important houses, such as those of Lord Grey of Wilton and Lord Dacre. He

LADY DACRE'S ALMSHOUSES—THE CHAPEL

LADY DACRE'S ALMS HOUSES—THE CHAPEL

speaks of the entry from it into Tothill Fields as being then called **Petty France**, in which were certain almshouses, twenty in number, together with a chapel, erected by one Cornelius van Dun, a Yeoman of the Guard to Henry VIII and his three successors. The mansion house of John Maunsel, in which he once entertained Henry III, his queen, and the King and Queen of Scotland, together with a large assembly of notables (so many, indeed, that tents and pavilions had to be erected as extra accommodation), was probably not far off in Tothill Fields, Stow merely calling it " his house in Totehill."

Tothill Street has changed out of all seeming within our memory. Before the Westminster Aquarium came into existence in 1876, and who among the older of us does not remember that amazing place, with its varied delights from Zazel perilously emerging out of her cannon and the Beckwiths living under water, to the interminable spot-*not*-barred billiard matches of Peal and Mitchell and the rest? Before, I say, this strange place came, with the Imperial Theatre that was added subsequently to its west end, there stood a collocation of quaint old houses with dormer windows and tiled roofs and so forth, the ground floors of which had long been converted into the inevitable shop-fronts. Well, they went in favour of the Aquarium; and in course of time that rather dreary, desolate relic of what seems to many of us like the Middle Ages, went too; and, as we know, great blocks of business premises stand on its site and the rotund dome of the Wesleyan Central Hall.

Crowther's drawing shows us one of these characteristic bits that formerly helped to preserve in this part an atmosphere of antiquity, an atmosphere hopelessly obliterated by the presence of the District Railway.

The little seventeenth-century house in the picture, with its tiled roof and attic dormer windows, its overhanging upper part, and the shop front of a later period which, however, falls so well into its scheme, stood, as we see, on the south side of Tothill Street just at its junction with Broadway, which thoroughfare is marked on the adjoining high brick building. It was, therefore, on or close to the site of the entrance to the District Railway station; and if one can visualize the absence of Queen Anne's Mansions, one will be able to realize what a charming vista this

23

as a rule larger) more impressive. The thoroughfare had a special relationship with old Westminster Bridge, since it was formed as an approach to that structure which Labeyle designed, and was opened simultaneously with it on 18th November 1750. Before this improvement was made, Birdcage Walk was only to be reached directly from what was then King Street, but is now the south end of Whitehall, by a narrow lane called George Yard, in which the George Inn was so important that it is specifically marked by Rocque in his plan of 1746.[1]

Great George Street formed a westerly continuation of Bridge Street, and the houses built in it were in the dignified style befitting the then important residential character of the neighbourhood—a character that may be judged from Kip's view of 1720. At the close of the eighteenth century Great George Street might have been distinctly described as being, in the words favoured by the older topographers, " well inhabited," and for many years later illustrious people like Lord Thurlow, Lord Macaulay, Daniel O'Connell, Lord Chancellor Hatherley, who died here so late as 1881, and was the last of such private residents, lived here, as Wilkes, and Lord Clare the friend of Goldsmith, and so forth had done at an earlier day. But not for these, not even for the Georgian dignity of its buildings, is the street remembered so much as for the fact that in one of its houses (No. 25 on the north side), then occupied by Sir Edward Knatchbull, the body of Lord Byron lay in state, as had, at an earlier day, the body of Sheridan in another of its residences. To-day such changes have taken place here that one may imagine the disconsolate ghosts of these two great men flitting aimlessly about the thoroughfare in a vain attempt to identify the last resting places of their corporeal entities. For the whole of the north side has been absorbed by the extension of the Government offices, and it is sometimes my privilege to go and waste the public time with a friend in the Ministry

---

[1] The fact that Westminster Bridge is shown in Rocque's map is, of course, accounted for by the Act for its construction having been passed in 1736, and the first stone having been laid on 29th January 1738-9, although it was not actually opened for traffic till 1750. Bridge Street was formed at the same time, the houses on its south side only being removed in 1867, although it is said that George III had suggested this improvement.

of Health whom I calculate must be sitting day after day in the exercise of his public labours (with which I interfere) on the spot where the great poet's body rested on its way from Missolonghi to Newstead.

Once the Institution of Civil Engineers had its headquarters on this very site, but when the Government required it, a new building was erected for the Engineers on the other side of the street, and again swept away more of the Georgian bricks and mortar. Indeed, there are only three or four of the old houses remaining in Great George Street to-day; and probably before long they, too, will disappear; and the last architectural links with the past will have been obliterated here. It should not be forgotten that that once very peripatetic institution, the National Portrait Gallery, now at anchor opposite St. Martin's-in-the-Fields, had its first resting place at 29 Great George Street, in 1859, when its contents numbered but fifty-six pictures!

Just before we reach Storey's Gate, on the north side of the thoroughfare, was a by-street known as Delahay Street. This no longer exists, having been swallowed up by official development. It contained some interesting old houses the backs of which looked on to the Park. In our day they had been converted to business uses, but once important people inhabited them as they did those of the longer and wider Duke Street, into which Delahay Street led. In 1874 both thoroughfares were known by the latter name.

Crowther has left a picture of the house of the most notorious, if not the most celebrated, inhabitant in the Duke Street portion of the thoroughfare. This was Lord Jeffreys, the redoubtable Lord Chief Justice, whose residence (by the side of which the narrower portion of the street led into Great George Street) was that facing us in the accompanying illustration. It was distinguished on its west side by a flight of stone steps into the Park, on which it immediately abutted. The privilege of having this entrance had been granted to Jeffreys by James II, although during one period of his life the judge could have had but little use for it, as we know that the King, in his almost pathetic anxiety for the safety of the Great Seal, concerning which he was superstitiously solicitous, insisted on Jeffreys living with his precious charge in special apartments strongly guarded at Whitehall. It was indeed soon after becoming

OLD ARCHWAY TENEMENT,
BROADWAY, WESTMINSTER

E

OLD ARCHWAY TENEMENT
BROADWAY, WESTMINSTER

OLD HOUSE AT THE CORNER OF TOTHILL STREET
AND BROADWAY

OLD HOUSE AT THE CORNER OF TOTHILL STREET
AND BROADWAY

Lord High Chancellor, in 1685, that Jeffreys rented the mansion here illustrated, from one Moses Pitt, a bookseller, and then described as " a great house in Duke Street just against the bird cages in St. James's Park." After Jeffreys' death his son inherited the house and occupied it until he was ruined by fast living. At a later period it was used as the headquarters of the Admiralty until that office was transferred, by William III, to Wallingford House. The Duke Street Chapel, as it was called, was converted to religious uses from the great hall of Jeffreys' house where, out of term time, he was accustomed to hear cases and administer many of his notorious judgments. It was on the north side of the residence and became a chapel, through the exertions of a Mr. Higgins and others, in 1709.

Among other former residents in Duke, or Delahay, Street were Matthew Prior, who lived in a house facing Charles Street, which thoroughfare led into Whitehall (the passage up steps from the Park, where Clive's statue is, marks it); Lord Orrery, the friend of Swift; and later, William Cobbett, in 1802; while Sir Isambard Brunel died here in 1849. When, too, Thomas Campbell the poet became connected with the Polish Association, he took chambers in Duke Street for the meetings of that body.

As one passes through Storey's Gate, leaving the red-brick building of the Institute of Mechanical Engineers (engineers and architects have absorbed Westminster it would seem), which marks the stairs named after the old Cockpit, on our left, we can pass across the Horse Guards Parade on our way to the Spring Gardens of which Crowther has left us several interesting pictures. On our way we cannot but cast a glance at that historic No. 10 Downing Street, where so much history has been made and which so many illustrious ones have successively inhabited. Its matured red-brick work and general simplicity of outline is curiously in contrast with the massive bulk of the Foreign Office, which Sir Gilbert Scott erected in 1867, and the old Horse Guards which John Vardy evolved from Kent's plans, in 1753. This latter structure, the squat proportions of which Hogarth once satirized, and Downing Street, and the buildings between them, help to preserve the former appearance of the area, in spite of the reconstructed Admiralty (a curiously inappropriate

27

piece of architecture in this connection), and as we look at it to-day we can recapture something of that Georgian atmosphere which has obliterated the Caroline convention that once dominated, and appropriately dominated (for it was Charles II who made St. James's Park, if not as it is, at least picturesque and loiterable), this spot.

And here it is, where the rebuilt Admiralty stands, with James II in bronze, and a howler in his Latin inscription, by the way, that once spread those Spring Gardens the name of which is still perpetuated in a tiny rebuilt corner of the area.

I have, in another book,[1] had something to say about these particular Spring Gardens (for there were several others in London at one time), and there is no necessity, therefore, for me to dwell on their earlier form and history here. Rather will it be interesting to note the changes that have occurred since Crowther made the beautiful water-colour drawings which accompany my text, at the spot where the gay Londoners of two centuries foregathered and amused themselves.

[1] *The Pleasure Haunts of London* (Constable and Co.).

JUDGE JEFFREYS' HOUSE, DELAHAY STREET, WESTMINSTER

CHAPTER III

SPRING GARDENS AND WHITEHALL

THE gradual development of the spot still known to us as Spring Gardens may be traced in that remarkable series of plans by which successive cartographers have indicated the growth of London. One of the earliest of these plans—that of Ralph Agas, dated *circa* 1560-70—shows the place as then being thickly wooded and divided from the Park by railings, the western boundary approximately coinciding with the present passage-way out of Cockspur Street. By 1658, when Faithorne produced his bird's-eye view of the city, houses are found to have replaced the trees, with a semicircular frontage to Charing Cross; the Spring Gardens, a formally laid-out space, divided from the Park by a stream over which was a small bridge connecting the two, being directly on the south of these buildings, as the Gardens had then been for many years, since, indeed, the reign of James I, when they were originally laid out. By Morden and Lea's map of 1682 we find further building development impinging on the Gardens which, however, were still of a certain size and character, although they had become greatly curtailed; while in Kip's view, dated *circa* 1710-20, they have disappeared entirely, their site being partly occupied by the private grounds of the adjoining houses and by the Park into which a portion seems to have been thrown.

The "way into the Park," shown by Kip, is the passage from Cockspur Street already referred to, which ran between two private gardens further south, and on which abutted what Kip calls "The Frans [French] Church," which stood approximately where the London County Council's old headquarters are now. When we reach Rocque's great plan of 1746, we find all this corner intersected by little byways, and the space behind the houses marked generically as Spring Gardens, although, as I have shown, the pleasure haunt which gave the name to

29

the area was considerably further to the south. It is interesting to note that in this plan an inn—The Mermaid—is first marked as being in the alley leading to Cockspur Street, whence the byway was at one time known as Mermaid Alley, and that to the north-west of the original Admiralty buildings, which were erected between 1722 and 1726, were some stables called Spring Gardens Mews. There is one other reference in this plan which, if we went by Rocque's spelling, might prove perplexing. Just at the spot where Whitehall begins to widen out into Charing Cross, a little north of Craig's Court, but on the west side, is an opening called Cromwell's Palace. This, however, is nothing more important than Cromwell Place, one of the numerous alleys that once existed here.

By the time Horwood produced his plan (1799) this byway, as well as another just to its south, known as Rummer's Court, had disappeared, new houses having been erected, and only the little Buckingham Court, once "a nest of dirt and vice," and a harbourage for Papists, immediately to the north of the Admiralty, remained; otherwise little change had taken place in the actual alignment of the buildings.

Rummer's Court took its name from the once well-known Rummer's Tavern, perpetuated by Hogarth in his "Night," and of which the Ship Tavern (later Restaurant) was a kind of lineal descendant. It was as famous a place of entertainment as the once well-known Lockitt's, which stood two doors away, on the site now occupied by Drummond's Bank.

Thus far we have been able approximately to visualize the appearance of Spring Gardens and its neighbourhood during Caroline and Georgian days. And if I were here only concerned with this immediate neighbourhood, so rich in historic and literary and artistic memories, I could fill pages with an account of the notable people who once lived hereabouts: Sir Philip Warwick at Warwick House (Warwick Street perpetuates his name) where, later, the Princess Charlotte resided and whence, on a famous occasion, she fled to Queen Caroline at Blackheath; the second Earl of Chesterfield, whose letters are less known than those of the fourth Earl but are full of interest; Sir William Morris and Prince Rupert, for instance. But these resided in what was called Outer Spring Gardens, to the west of the little passage-way from

30

SPRING GARDENS FROM THE MALL

Cockspur Street to the Park. Others who lived in the portion which more immediately concerns us here were Lord Crofts, the " mad lord," as he was called, whose domicile was described as " in the place commonly called the old Spring Gardens " (that was when the New Spring Gardens at Vauxhall had put this earlier one out of fashion); Sir Edward Hungerford, who came here in 1681, when he had given up his mansion in the Strand, where Hungerford Market and later the Charing Cross Railway Station were to come; Colley Cibber, who was living, from 1711 to 1714, at his house near the Bull Head Tavern (on part of the site of Drummond's Bank), next door to which hostelry Milton once lodged at the house of a Mr. Thomson; down to the days of George Canning, who was at a house at the corner of Cockspur Street in 1799. Two famous architects were also residents here at other periods: Sir Robert Taylor, who died " at his residence in Spring Gardens " in 1788; and Sir George Gilbert Scott, who came to No. 20, in 1838, and kept the premises as his offices (when he went to St. John's Wood to live) during his lifetime. But the first of Crowther's pictures claims more specific notice. It shows us the passage-way from the Park to Cockspur Street as it was just over forty years ago.

Even a Londoner, familiar as he may be with the varied and ever occurring changes in his city, will find it difficult, I think, to reconstruct this area to-day from what it appeared like even so relatively recently as the 'nineties of the last century. The difference will appear more marked in the succeeding illustrations, but even in this one (*vide Plate*) we are confronted with a structure whose outlines we have quite forgotten, although it is at a spot which remains essentially the same. For while the passage-way itself and the building on the left, till recently occupied by the London County Council, are familiar, that on the right has gone and in its place is a portion of the Admiralty Arch buildings which now abut immediately on the footway, which has been widened since the time when it was but a narrow passage with iron gates the exiguousness of which once produced a characteristic quip from no less a person than Canning (who, as we have seen, once lived in Spring Gardens) himself. On one occasion a lady asked him why they had made the iron gates here so narrow. " Well, you see," he replied, " such very fat people tried to get

PASSAGE IN SPRING GARDENS FROM TRAFALGAR SQUARE TO THE MALL

begins; the wall shown being a continuation of that in the former picture (*vide Plate*). The buildings within this enclosure have now become part and parcel of the Admiralty Arch. Like Augustus at Rome we found London all brick and we are making it all stone, so that we no longer have the mellow colouring of these old Georgian houses to give to and take beauty from, the surrounding foliage. Indeed, all that greenery is gone too; and there is gone with it a feature which was for long an attractive one at this spot and one which Crowther has included on the extreme right of his picture, the shed where the old lady sold fresh milk from the cow; she was a successor in that occupation of Mrs. Searle, Brummell's aunt, to whom that young gentleman, up from Eton, was paying a visit when he encountered the Duchess of Rutland and the Prince of Wales—a meeting that coloured the whole of his subsequent life.

It will surprise many who do not remember Spring Gardens in their earlier state to learn that once its purlieus contained two chapels. Concerning one of these the information is somewhat vague. All we know is that it was a French Protestant place of worship; but when it was erected or by whom is, I believe, not recorded. We are told, however, that on 2nd December 1716 it was found to be on fire, a circumstance which " occasioned great alarm in the neighbourhood from its vicinity to several depositories of gunpowder." The fire, however, owing to the exertions of the authorities (George, Prince of Wales, taking a leading part), was prevented from spreading, although the chapel itself must have been destroyed, as we hear that a new one was erected on its site by the Hon. Edward Southwell, Secretary of State for Ireland, in 1731. As this new building was intended for the use of the inhabitants, it is evident that the French Protestants found a religious domicile elsewhere. This chapel stood on the site of old Berkeley House (where, as we have seen, the London County Council buildings now are), and is clearly shown in Kip's plan of 1710-20, as is the new built structure in that of Rocque (1746), where it is marked by name. This disposes of the suggestion made by J. Holden Macmichael, the historian of Charing Cross and its neighbourhood, that it was probably identical with the other chapel once in existence in Spring Gardens.

ST. MATTHEW'S CHAPEL, SPRING GARDENS

city. None of them remains to-day. Rebuilding essentially altered this part; but still more has the opening up of the Mall created an atmosphere entirely alien from what existed even at the time when Crowther was intent on pictorially preserving what he had but too good reason to know would, in the near future, disappear. There was here, in our own day, the tall building of the National Bank, flanked on the east by Messrs. Stanford's premises; while two doors to the west was a quaint Georgian front, with rounded windows about the spot where the once well-known British Coffee House, much resorted to by Scotch visitors, stood. The interesting model, by Mr. John B. Thorp (now in the London Museum), gives an excellent idea of what the houses on this site some three centuries earlier looked like.

Collectors of prints are no doubt familiar with a lithograph executed by George Scharf, and entitled " Fancy Fair at Governor Penn's house in Spring Gardens," 1830. This John Penn was a descendant of the founder of Pennsylvania, and at this very house depicted by Scharf carried on that curious club known as the Outinian Society, which he had inaugurated, in 1818, at 190 Piccadilly. It was by way of being a matrimonial society, and had for its object the strengthening of the marriage bond. How long it went on for I am unable to say; but in Scharf's picture we see the members enjoying themselves *al fresco* in the gardens behind 10 New Street, a thoroughfare that then ran at right angles from Spring Gardens towards the Park. If the ladies and gentlemen depicted in close and even loving propinquity were all hus-bands and wives, Penn might well have congratulated himself on the success of his scheme.

As in following Crowther's drawings we shall have occasion to visit one or two spots in Whitehall before proceeding along the Strand, we may conveniently reach that area by retracing a portion of our steps, and going across Horse Guards Parade. As we do so we shall pass the spot where once stood what was called the Gun House; a landmark that forms the subject of another of our artist's drawings. This structure was built of red-brick and stood on the north side of the Horse Guards Parade. It took its name from the fact that the elaborate piece of ordin-ance captured from Soult, after the battle of Salamanca, was placed in

35

front of it.[1] This gun, I may parenthetically remind the reader, was presented to the Prince Regent, and it is said that when he came to Lon-London, Soult smilingly recognized it; it now occupies a position on the south side of the parade ground. There was practically no ornamental attraction about the Gun House, except that the brackets of the overdoor were carved, and thus gave a touch of elegance (to use a word much beloved by the period) to what was otherwise solid but plain. Behind the house were the residences known as Spring Gardens Terrace, the upper portions of which appear in Crowther's picture. These, together with the Gun House itself, were pulled down for the extension of the Admiralty buildings which now cover their sites.

As, following in Crowther's footsteps, our next objective is the Almonry, which stood in the precincts of Whitehall Palace, we may reach that spot by going through the Horse Guards (not forgetting to set our watches by its immaculate clock, as Ferdinand suggested doing to Mr. Glastonbury), and across the street once spanned by Holbein's Gateway, whence Charles I went to his doom at Whitehall—mounting the steps, as Lord Pembroke saw him, in the Horse Guards which communicated with the gateway; or we can make a slight détour (which will be worth while) by passing through Treasury Passage, of the existence of which so many are unaware, which runs into the east end of Downing Street, by the beautiful old Treasury, on Horse Guards Parade, erected in 1733 from Kent's designs—designs that once embraced a far larger structure. Originally a building dating from the time of Henry VIII occupied this site (it is clearly shown in the seventeenth-century picture by Danckerts), and in this passage to-day can be seen a large window with mullions and transom and, opposite, a two-light window, both surrounded by Tudor brickwork and obviously incorporated from the older building into Kent's work. It was just behind the Treasury that the royal cockpit stood with its octagonal roof, in which the cock-fighting of Tudor days had given place to the dramatic performances of those of the Stuarts,

[1] It is a curious fact that in a picture of the Horse Guards by S. Scott, who was living *circa* 1710-72, an earlier gun is shown in front of this very house, and it may have been from this one that the name was originally given it.

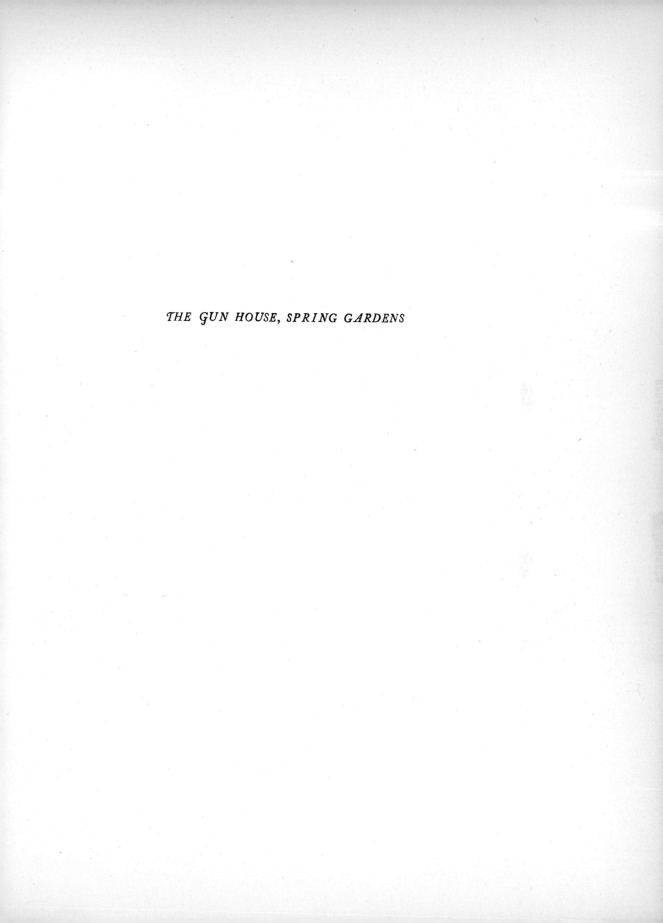

THE GUN HOUSE, SPRING GARDENS

THE GUN HOUSE, SPRING GARDENS

and to musical ones in the time of Cromwell, with a surprising political *finale* during the Georgian period.

Without the aid of plans and very ample space on which to spread one's description it is difficult to indicate what Whitehall (by which word I mean not merely the large inchoate palace, but all this area) looked like in past times. As we walk along the wide thoroughfare with practically nothing but the Banqueting Hall remaining of the palace, it is almost impossible to realize the period when the precincts of that palace stretched from the river edge to the Horse Guards Parade; when the roadway between Holbein's Gateway (stretching across the street from where Dover House is now) and the King Street Gateway (which stood just to the north of Downing Street), was incorporated in the palace precincts; when the old Treasury we have just passed was represented in Charles II's day by the Duke of Albemarle's lodgings; when the famous Stone Gallery (where Pepys used to see Charles walking and used to converse with the Duke of York) ran, north to south, through Montagu House; when the Privy Garden (where the same impressionable, delightful creature was once so pleased to see Lady Castlemaine's smocks hanging out to dry) covered the site of the buildings and much else, on the north of the Banqueting Hall; and when the Bowling Green where Charles I so often diverted himself at his favourite game covered the site of Richmond Terrace. The United Service Institute occupies the ground where the Palace Gateway stood, and Horse Guards Avenue runs through the sites of the Great Hall and the Chapel. It seems almost incredible that so rash and rambling a structure as Whitehall Palace should have shrunk to such tiny proportions; that the only relic of it to which we can point is that beautiful one the façade of which is the most graceful and dignified we have to show in London, and which was, after all, not an original portion of the palace at all, but a specimen, as it were, of that far more grandiose structure which Inigo Jones designed, but which the civil troubles prevented from materializing.

The Almonry of Crowther's drawing was quite close to the northern boundary of the palace, for it stood immediately at that side of the Palace Stairs or landing-stage to the river which, by the way, is not to be confounded with the Privy Stairs which were considerably to the south, in a direct line from Dover House.

As is generally known, the office of the Hereditary Grand Almoner, together with that of the High Almoner, was originally in the Royal Palace of Whitehall itself, where its officials held their deliberations in a specially allocated part of that vast building. This has sometimes been confounded with the other Almonry, or Ambry, as it was occasionally, but incorrectly, called, which stood off Tothill Street, at the east end of Great Sanctuary, and where alms, collected in the Abbey, were distributed, and, by the way, Caxton first set up his famous printing-press.

The Almonry, of which Crowther has left us a drawing, was that instituted for the dissemination of the royal charities, and in the year 1820 its activities were removed to an old house which then stood a little to the north of Fife House, immediately north of Whitehall Stairs and west of the United Service Museum. From a photograph taken before 1870 we can see what this structure looked like in those days, when nothing intervened between it and the river but an exiguous piece of walled-in garden, in which the sub-almoner grew flowers of which, we are told, he was justly proud.

The appearance of the house obviously indicated that it had been erected on ancient foundations, for its lower portion was of stone, and in it was an arched entrance which had doubtless once served as a water-gate. Another old feature was a mullioned window; and as, in a plan dated 1680, the premises on the site occupied later by the Almonry are described as " the Small Beer Buttery," the inference is that the more ancient portion of the building was a relic of this.

When the Victoria Embankment was in process of formation, from 1862 to 1870, this interesting and picturesque old structure was partly demolished; and the Almonry Office was removed to 36 Spring Gardens. Crowther's drawing was executed in 1884, and a comparison with the photograph of 1870, to which I have already referred, shows with what accuracy every detail has been produced, and what an artistic *motif* the painter was able to make of his subject. The large scaffold-surrounded structure on the right was a portion of the Government buildings then in course of re-erection.

38

THE ALMONRY OFFICE, WHITEHALL

THE ALMONRY OFFICE, WHITEHALL

If you turn to Wheatley's monumental development of Cunningham's *Handbook to London*, known to all students of the city's topography as *London Past and Present*, you are likely to be disappointed at the meagre description there given of Whitehall Yard, for all it has to say about it is this: "Whitehall Yard, north of the Chapel Royal (Banqueting House). Here is the Royal United Service Institution, but a great change has been made in the yard lately by reason of the demolition of houses, and the erection of a large range of mansions on the river side." Why the one fact about the place mentioned by Cunningham to the effect that in it (in 1849) was the office of the Comptroller-General of the Exchequer, containing an ancient chair on which the Lord High Treasurer used to sit, was discarded in Dr. Wheatley's amplification I do not know; nor why something more precise concerning the changes that had later come over this spot was not set forth. For instance, we might have been told that it was in this very office, then at No. 3 Whitehall Yard, that the ceremony known as "The Trial of the Pyx" which, according to Herbert, in his book on *The City Companies*, is "an investigation or enquiry into the purity and weight of the money coined, before the Lords of the Council, aided by the professional knowledge of a jury of the Goldsmiths' Company," and known even so early as the days of Edward I as a then well-known custom, used to take place, before it was removed to the Hall of the Goldsmiths' Company. Again, at No. 6 Whitehall Yard, the Army Medical Board had its office. Before 1895, too, the Royal United Service Institution, which had been founded in Whitehall Yard in 1830, had its entrance here, although in that year the museum was transferred to the Banqueting House, and an additional wing for it was erected adjoining the north side of the relic of Inigo Jones's projected palace.

The erection of the War Office and the formation of Horse Guards Parade have essentially altered the appearance of this corner of Whitehall, and it is only by such pictorial documents as Crowther and others have left us that we can easily visualize the appearance of such special spots in London's vast organism.

In the plan of Whitehall, dated 1680, we see that Scotland Yard consisted of two large spaces divided by residences, considerably to the

39

WHITEHALL YARD

Vanbrugh's House in the background

SPRING GARDENS AND WHITEHALL

picture were, according to a note made by him, " shortly to be pulled
down "; and to-day Whitehall Court and the War Office cast their
vast shadows over the site of Vanbrugh's toy house.[1]

Indeed, the former covers the area on which it stands; while Horse
Guards Avenue now runs in front (where the tree is shown) from east to
west; and Whitehall Court is rather to the back of the building on the
right. Of these buildings not all were destroyed, as that with the
portico in the immediate foreground still remains as does the structure
on the left, with its doorway approached by steps. Railings, however,
divide these from the roadway, which has been sunk so as to leave them
on a sort of terrace.

[1] As the dates and architects' names of our great buildings seldom seem to be remembered, I may note here that the War Office was erected in 1906, from the designs of
Mr. William Young, and that the new Scotland Yard was the work of Norman Shaw,
and arose in 1891.

41   G

picture were, according to a note made by him, " shortly to be pulled down "; and to-day Whitehall Court and the War Office cast their vast shadows over the site of Vanbrugh's toy house.[1]

Indeed, the former covers the area on which it stands; while Horse Guards Avenue now runs in front (where the tree is shown) from east to west; and Whitehall Court is rather to the back of the building on the right. Of these buildings not all were destroyed, as that with the portico in the immediate foreground still remains as does the structure on the left, with its doorway approached by steps. Railings, however, divide these from the roadway, which has been sunk so as to leave them on a sort of terrace.

[1] As the dates and architects' names of our great buildings seldom seem to be remembered, I may note here that the War Office was erected in 1906, from the designs of Mr. William Young, and that the new Scotland Yard was the work of Norman Shaw, and arose in 1891.

CHAPTER IV

THE STRAND

WHEN Crowther made his drawing of the west end of the Strand in 1880, the chief change that had occurred there in then recent days had taken place some five years previously, with the demolition of Northumberland House. What a feature that historic pile was at this spot can be realized by an examination of the innumerable pictures and prints of it. It gave a dignity to the western entrance of London's most historically important thoroughfare, and fittingly inaugurated that series of private palaces which, at an earlier day, had lined the street, but which, with this solitary exception, had long disappeared. It is here only necessary to say a few words about this famous landmark. It had been originally erected by Bernard Jansen and Gerard Christmas, for the first Earl of Northampton, about 1605. The Earl left it to his nephew, the Earl of Suffolk, whose name it bore till 1658, although it had become the property of the Percy family, through marriage, some sixteen years before that date. It was in 1642 that Algernon, Earl of Northumberland, caused a river front, completing the quadrangle, to be built by Inigo Jones; and what the house looked like with this addition may be seen by the drawing Hollar made of it, now in the Pepysian Library at Cambridge. In course of time many changes and modifications took place in the building; the two pepper-pot towers on the river side were taken down; Mylne added a wing and pavilion in 1765, and Adam a drawing-room nine years later, besides doing much internal reconstruction. So that as it came down to us in the nineteenth century the principal façade retained its Jacobean character, although the river front had become entirely Georgian, with the still later additions of a balcony protected by an iron canopy. When the scheme for forming a roadway from Trafalgar Square to the Embankment had been passed, compulsory powers were sought and obtained

OLD HOUSES IN THE STRAND, NEXT TO THE ADELPHI THEATRE

from Parliament for the purchase of the mansion, and the Duke of North-umberland of the day received half a million pounds for the property in the June of 1874. The place was then dismantled, three million bricks being disposed of, besides four hundred tons of lead; the great marble staircase being subsequently removed to 49 Prince's Gate, and the splendid contents being distributed between Alnwick, No. 2 Grosvenor Place, which had then become the new London residence of the family, and Syon House, on whose roof the historic lion (which had been cast by Carter from the designs of Laurent Delvaux in 1752) lashes his tail as it had long done in the sight of curious and interested Londoners.

The subsequent formation of Northumberland Avenue, which so entirely altered the alignment of the thoroughfare at this spot, together with the purchase of certain adjoining shops, cost £150,000. It was opened in March 1876, and many years ago a writer on London remarked that " for its length the street is disproportionately wide, and the excessive width and the rounding off of the angles renders the Trafalgar Square end one of the most dangerous street-corners in London for foot-passengers." This was written over thirty years since, and as the authorities do not seem to have considered underground passages are as needful here as they are opposite the Mansion House, the danger, as we are all aware, has been increased tenfold with the coming of the motorbus and taxicab.

With the exception of the disappearance of Northumberland House the entrance to the Strand has altered less than might have been expected in these days of drastic rebuilding. The presence (although how long it will remain it is impossible to say) of the block once comprising Morley's Hotel (the Golden Cross—a survival of the earlier one here and the still earlier one which occupied approximately the centre of the row of houses then standing where the Nelson monument is now) is responsible for this to some extent; but still more so is the fact that Trafalgar Square retains much the same appearance (except for the addition of certain statues and so forth) as it did when it was completed by Sir Charles Barry in 1841; although to be sure the Nelson monu-ment was not actually finished till some eight years later; the four lions not coming from Landseer's studio for another eighteen years.

43

It may not be within some people's knowledge that the capital of the column is of bronze recovered from the wreck of the "Royal George," while elsewhere in the Square the statue of George IV by Chantrey (the last instalment of the cost for which was not paid till *after* the sculptor's death) was originally intended for the top of the Marble Arch when that monument stood in front of Buckingham Palace. Trafalgar Square itself is not largely changed, nor indeed except for its flanking buildings is it capable of change. The premises of the Union Club have been wholly reconstructed it is true, and the adjoining College of Physicians, the entrance of which is in Pall Mall East, has put on a new stone dress. Some shops which abutted immediately on the west end of the National Gallery have been removed; and those in Cockspur Street have been almost entirely rebuilt; while the entrance into the Mall has added what, but for the too massive nature of the Admiralty Arch, would have been a glorious vista and forms, after all, a pleasant peep into the greenery of the Park.

Such alterations may be regarded on the whole as improvements, and they are such as have occurred since Crowther made his drawing in 1880.

When, however, we leave the Square which Chantrey once said was " the most favourable that could be found or imagined for any work of art," and which Sir Robert Peel asserted to be " one of the finest sites in Europe," we shall find many changes in the appearance of the Strand as we proceed eastwards; changes that have taken place, I mean, since 1887, when Crowther executed the next picture in the series here dealt with. Of course, the most marked of these alterations had occurred some twenty-four years earlier, when old Hungerford Market gave place to Charing Cross Railway Station, and Barry erected his vast hotel and laid out the station yard on the site of Market Street (leading to the Market) and the old shops and houses which are shown flanking it on both sides by Tallis, in his *London Street Views* of 1838. The presence of a large semi-official building such as Charing Cross Station may be said to be, so dominates the area in which it finds itself that lesser changes seem, by comparison, almost negligible. And yet, if we look more closely, a variety of these will appear to have taken place. For instance,

OLD HOUSES IN THE STRAND, EAST END
OF ST. MARY'S CHURCH

OLD HOUSES IN THE STRAND

East end of St. Mary's Church

practically all the shops have been either rebuilt or reconstructed. Messrs. Coutts's bank has entirely disappeared, and with the widening of the thoroughfare its site now exhibits the red-brick, stone-faced range of buildings which, I imagine, it is complacently felt reproduce the Adams convention at the spot which "the Adelphi" once created into a building site on the artificial foundations of their daring contrivance. This widening was begun by the setting back of the roadway just to the east of where the Tivoli Cinema stands in its classic isolation. The coming of this new feature was responsible for the destruction of one of those tentacles into the Strand from the Adelphi which served as outposts of the Adams development; and that which perilously hangs on to life at the opposite side of Adam Street and forms the west corner of the block still jutting into the street, will disappear before long in order to afford a uniform width to the Strand at this point.

But this takes us away from Crowther's picture, which he calls " The Strand, next the Adelphi Theatre," and which is what here specially concerns us. The Adelphi Theatre itself, originally known as the Sans Pareil, was erected by a certain Mr. John Scott, a colour maker, who seems to have had dramatic tendencies, and was first opened on 27th November 1806. It was apparently the histrionic talents of his daughter that induced Scott to embark on theatrical management, as that lady's recitations and so forth were for long a standing dish and a profitable attraction at the little playhouse. In 1825 Terry and Yates took over the place, the former being backed in his venture by his friend Sir Walter Scott. Later came Charles Mathews, the elder, who gave here his famous " At Homes." In 1858 Benjamin Webster, who had succeeded Yates, rebuilt the theatre from the designs of Thomas Wyatt; and just thirty years later, while Crowther was making his sketch, the Strand front was widened and completely reconstructed. The Adelphi stood on the site of No. 411 Strand, and but one house separated it from Nos. 413 and 414, the beautiful old premises which Crowther has reproduced. In 1838 the former of these was occupied by one Price, a fishmonger, and in recent days it was an " Oyster and Supper Rooms "; while No. 414 was still a cigar merchant's, as it had been when Queen Victoria came to the throne. Behind them is Heathcock Court, with an entrance

the left (but out of the picture) was Denny's, which inaugurated that series of bookshops from which Holywell took its alternative name of Booksellers' Row. The Charing Cross Road is a poor substitute for this quaint old thoroughfare where one loved to loiter, and in which, by the way, I personally never saw a cab—a sedan chair would, after all, have been far more in the picture.

The two old houses in the Strand (Nos. 166-7), which are gone, marked what had been known as " Golden Buildings," which lay behind them, in Strand Lane. What gave its name to these " Buildings " is unknown, although, as there was a sign of " Ye Golden Ball " near Strand Bridge (at the Strand end of the Lane), on a token issued by one John Stationer, this may have had something to do with it—either as cause or effect. There was, too, an advertisement dated 1699, which indicated that No. 165 was then occupied by " Inglis's warehouse for Scot's Pills," which short cuts to health were, we are further informed, " Sold by J. Inglis, now living at the Golden Unicorn over against ye May Pole in ye Strand." In 1893 Nos. 166-7 were demolished; and in the case of the latter this was specially regrettable as the architraves of the windows were surrounded by carving which gave its frontage a specially effective appearance.

Of Golden Buildings Crowther luckily made the sketch here reproduced, and thus, although they were pulled down soon after he did so, we can see what the tenements in it looked like owing to his anticipation of their imminent fate and his artistic and accurate skill. They occupied a portion of Strand Lane, the subject of another of the drawings, concerning which it is convenient to say something here, although for the moment it carries us rather out of our direct itinerary.

Strand Lane was originally known as Strand Bridge Lane, because it was arched in former times by a bridge, and ran down to a landing-stage on the Thames. It was a street of great antiquity, and is mentioned by Stow; while Strype amplifies the earlier topographer's description of it by informing us that " in the high street in the Strand there was a fair bridge, called Strand-bridge, and under it a way or lane to the waterside; which said lane is yet remaining, but nothing remains of the bridge but that the place yet retains the name." He adds that " here is a Watch-

STRAND LANE

Looking North

STRAND LANE, LOOKING TOWARDS THE RIVER

H

instance, the low shed-like structures on the left are no longer there, a long blank wall being in their place; and, above all, no longer is there the projecting upper portion supported by a single iron pole of the house on the right, which was entered by a flight of half a dozen stone steps, and which is now represented by a warehouse-like building. One can still enter Surrey Street from Surrey Steps, as they were called (shown in Horwood's plan as being between Nos. 30 and 31), but the post and handrail indicated just below the bracket lamp that once lighted it are no longer there, the steps being widened and painfully sophisticated. The old cobbled way, too, has given place to paving stones. What was once a thoroughfare from the Strand,[1] although a narrow enough one, is now but a path for the few pedestrians who make use of it to visit the Roman Bath; for the once short cut to the Embankment is no longer in existence, the lower end of the lane being flanked by a low brick wall surmounted by an iron railing.

The other view (which, by the way, Crowther executed in 1880) represents the continuation of Strand Lane to the river, and is specially interesting as indicating the old houses which once stood on its east side just below the steps into Surrey Street. As will be seen, the second one on the left had a quite important doorway, indicating a private residence of some character. The upper portion of the house had, however, been removed, and an iron railing guards (as we see) what had become the lowered roof of the structure—a roof obviously used for some special purpose—perhaps as a drying-place for washing. On the west side of the street was once the Strand Inn, and I am inclined to think that the low sheds on the right of Crowther's picture (they are more clearly indicated in the former one—No. 24) were part of its premises. In early days there was a landing-stage to the river at the bottom of the Lane (it is mentioned by Stow); but there is now no way on to the Embankment, and in the picture the end of the street is shown boarded up. The campanile in the distance is the Shot Tower, near the Surrey end of Waterloo Bridge, erected in 1789 in connection with Messrs. Watts's manufactory, and still a prominent object rising from the dilapidated

[1] The Strand has been raised some twenty feet at this point, and therefore there was formerly no need for the steps which now lead from it to Strand Lane.

49

wharves of the south bank of the river. To-day it is difficult to realize that one is in this once picturesque alley, for great warehouse-like structures rise along the whole of its west side, and the place wears a desolate air and, what is worse, a sordid one.

I have been led by the association of certain old houses at this spot with those in the more westerly part of the Strand, and thus, indirectly, to Golden Buildings and Strand Lane, out of the strict itinerary it is useful to follow in dealing with Crowther's drawings, and we must therefore return to Cecil Street, at the bottom of which, facing the river, once stood the curious old residence for many years occupied by Sir William Congreve, the inventor of the famous rocket that goes by his name.

Cecil Street, as well as Salisbury Street, which ran approximately where old Salisbury or Cecil House, built by Elizabeth's " little great Secretary ' at the beginning of the seventeenth century, had formerly stood, has been obliterated by the immense block of the Hotel Cecil. This huge caravanserai was erected by Jabez Balfour and his company soon after the year 1888, in which Lord Salisbury sold this portion of his property for £200,000. How markedly it altered the appearance of the Strand can be realized by comparing the present thoroughfare at this spot with pictures of what it was at an earlier day. Just fifty years before the sale took place Tallis produced his remarkable *London Street Views*, and in the one dealing with this area will be seen a faithful delineation of the shops which existed between Cecil Street and Salisbury Street, where now the double entrances to the Hotel are. Both the tributary thorough-fares have been obliterated, and it is by narrow ways and steps only that you can now reach the river at this spot.

At the beginning of the nineteenth century Cecil Street was lined with houses on both sides, and was fairly wide, although it had a bottle-necked narrow entrance into the Strand. Its houses were numbered 1 to 12, going south on the west side, and 13 to 26 going north on the east side. At this time Dr. Woolaston, the noted physician, was living in No. 18, and Spranger Barry, the actor, died here; rather later Edmund Kean came to lodge in a garret here, at No. 21; while next door, No. 20, Carey, the translator of Dante, was residing in 1816; and

SIR WILLIAM CONGREVE'S HOUSE, SOUTH END OF CECIL STREET,
STRAND

Dickens had lodgings in the street in 1833. The house at the south-west end of the thoroughfare, occupied by Sir William Congreve, was No. 12; and what it looked like during his time can be seen by Crowther's picture. What is not, of course, seen is the very different aspect of the river frontage in pre-Embankment days when the Thames laved, at high tide, the bases of buildings now far removed from its reach, or left a deposit of mud, at low water, such as may be seen on the south bank to-day. Wharves and sheds and so forth then lined the river-side on the north bank, and at the end of Cecil Street, between Congreve's House and the water, was Mr. Capper's Wharf. Congreve's[1] residence is shown in a panoramic view of London from the river, dated 1849, and is there marked " Congreve House," so either its owner must have called it this, or his fame must have been sufficient in his own day for his residence so to be named in a print of London which only marks, in this way, outstanding and important buildings.

Few more extraordinary looking houses than that of Congreve could have been remaining in London when Crowther executed his water-colour drawing of it in 1882. It altogether defies architectural definition, and it is lucky we have this excellent representation, as a written description is therefore unnecessary. The structure seems to have been built up piecemeal on the foundation of an old building indicated by the arched doorway on the left. The first floor and the turret on the right were of wood, the former surmounted by a covered balcony of essentially early Victorian character; an interesting feature being the projecting window, on the right of the house, surmounted by a semicircular balcony. The red-brick erection at the south-east corner of the street was obviously of much later date; and the funnel-like entrance to the Strand which led by a passage under the houses into that thoroughfare, is clearly seen in the drawing. In Horwood's plan (1799) houses are shown on the right extending down to the same frontage as Congreve's, but these had been cleared away and an open space guarded by railings formed in their place. The Embankment Gardens in front of the two great hotels now cover all this area.

[1] The other William Congreve, it will be remembered, lived once in Surrey Street, and was there visited, on a notable occasion, by Voltaire.

Close by, but rather to the west of Salisbury Street, was one of those many piers or wharves which dotted the river bank before bridges were as numerous as they are now, and whence people took boat for the opposite shore or for pleasure excursions on the Thames. This one was known as Ivy Bridge, and the way to it from the Strand was by a passage called Ivy, or Ivy Bridge, Lane. What this lane looked like in 1882 may be seen from Crowther's drawing; what is now in its place we all know. Tallis marks it as a little alley running between Nos. 75 and 76 Strand. It actually formed part of that block of buildings which still projects into the Strand awaiting the pick of destruction which will enable the buildings to be set back in a line with those on each side of it. The memory of Ivy Bridge Lane is, however, worth preserving, for it is a byway of much antiquity. Ivy Bridge carried the roadway over " a way under it leading down to the Thames," as mentioned by Stow: and here the same authority tells us was the division between the Liberty of the Duchy of Lancaster and Westminster.

In this connection it is worth remembering that the word bridge, as associated with such byways as Ivy Lane and Strand Lane, denoted not a bridge by the river, but one which then carried the traffic along the Strand, as indicated by Stow's description here quoted. The same authority tells us that in his day this bridge had been removed, but that " the lane remaineth as afore or better." However, this improvement did not last, for Strype, in the eighteenth century, speaks of the lane as being " now very bad and scarce fit for use, by reason of the unpassableness of the way." It seems that when Salisbury Street, just to the east, was formed on the site of Salisbury House, the *raison d'être* of Ivy Lane as a passage to the river ceased to exist, in the same way that Strand Bridge and pier gave way to the better accommodation of Salisbury Stairs. However, the lane, exiguous and dirty as it undoubtedly was, once served a prince's purpose; for when the young James, Duke of York, fled from his father's foes, on 20th April 1648, he made his way down it, accompanied by Bamfield, his confessor, to the boat awaiting him at the landing-stage at its end. Crowther's picture is taken from the Strand end of Ivy Lane, and is dated 1882, at a time when, although many of the old buildings surrounding it remained, here and there

IVY BRIDGE LANE, STRAND, LOOKING SOUTH

IVY BRIDGE LANE, STRAND

Looking South

altered by reconstruction, the footway itself was bricked and in comparison with what it must have been in Strype's time was relatively clean and certainly passable. The inscription over the archway indicates that it was still called Ivy Bridge Lane.

We must for a moment cross the Strand in order to visit the site of Exchange Court, or Alley, of which Crowther made his picture in 1882. The byway took its name from Exeter 'Change, and in common with that mart, as well as Exeter and Burleigh Streets, was formed on the site of the gardens of old Exeter House. Horwood calls it 'Change Alley, and it ran behind Exeter 'Change, being reached from the Strand by Burleigh Street, from which it branched off on the right-hand side and then turned due north into Exeter Street; thus being partly parallel and partly at right-angles with Exeter 'Change, which abutted immediately on the east of Burleigh Street. Crowther's drawing shows the old houses (in the background) which were still here till 1882, when he made it. The modern structures in the foreground help to accentuate the picturesqueness of these survivals. On the right is, however, an old-fashioned shop-front with reflectors over the windows; and the wooden bench on the left helps to give an air of familiarity to the little courtyard. There was probably a tavern close by. The small opening at the back led into Exeter Street.

By the way, there was another alley, sometimes called Exchange Alley, further west, which led directly from the Strand to Maiden Lane, just to the east of Bedford Street. This should be, as it is correctly termed by Horwood, *New* Exchange Alley, and took its name from the New Exchange, or Britain's Bourse, as it was alternatively called, on the opposite (south) side of the Strand, and for many years perpetuated the memory of that building in which James I had taken an interest and among whose later memories was that of the " White Milliner "—the Duchess of Tyrconnel who, having fallen on bad times, supported herself by this trade, but to hide her identity always appeared at her stall in a white mask and gown.[1]

Hatton, writing in 1708, describes Norfolk Street, to which we must

[1] Douglas Jerrold, in 1840, wrote a play on the subject, entitled *The White Milliner,* it will be remembered.

transfer ourselves, passing, on the way, the drastic changes that have entirely altered the Strand since those days and indeed from what most of us once knew it, as " a very pleasant, regular, and spacious street." It had not been many years before Hatton wrote, that the residence of the Howards stood on this spot; indeed, Norfolk Street and the other thoroughfares adjacent were formed about 1682. When the first quarter of the eighteenth century closed Norfolk Street had become a fashionable place of abode, and Seymour speaks of it then as being " esteemed the best both for buildings and pleasantness of a prospect into the Thames." In 1724 an Act was passed to enable the Duke of Norfolk " to make leases for 60 years " in the streets on his Strand property.

To-day there has been so much rebuilding here, especially notice-able in the red-brick gothic structures facing the Embankment, that the old-world *aura* has quite disappeared, and only the ghosts (if they walk) of William Penn, who once lived in No. 21, where the Arundel Hotel, here commemorated by Crowther, was to come, and where, in the interim, Dr. Brocklesby lived; or that of " Downright " Shippen, the one in-corruptible of his day, according to Sir Robert Walpole; or of Samuel Ireland, with his son of Shakespearean forgeries notoriety, who once lived at No. 8, can conjure back a period which is gradually receding into the mists of relative antiquity. In spite of these, and of Dr. Birch, the antiquary, and Spranger Barry, the actor, Mortimer, the painter, and Henry Thomas Buckle, and gentle Miss Mitford who used to stay at No. 35, the street, will always be chiefly associated with William Mount-fort, actor and playwright, not only because he lodged in a house on the east side of the thoroughfare, two doors beyond Howard Street, but because it was at the junction of these ways that he was set on and murdered by the notorious Lord Mohun and his confederate, Captain Hill, on 9th December 1692, opposite the residence of Mrs. Brace-girdle. One ought not to forget, amid the glamour of such names, the fact that perhaps the two most notable past inhabitants of Norfolk Street were Sir Roger de Coverley and Mrs. Lirriper, as we have the unim-peachable authority of Mr. Addison, Sir Richard Steele, and Mr. Charles Dickens for knowing. Howard Street, linking up Norfolk Street with Arundel Street, has also its tale of memorable inhabitants,

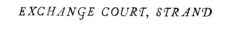

EXCHANGE COURT, STRAND

EXCHANGE COURT, STRAND

for here lived Congreve before he moved to Surrey Street, and after he had left Southampton Street; and here Mrs. Bracegirdle was his neighbour. The main feature in Crowther's picture is the large corner building, No. 12, which was formerly the residence of the Earls of Dysart, but had been for some years previously to its demolition carried on as the Dysart Hotel. Its most picturesque feature was the projecting bay window, and the room which it lighted contained much excellent panelling, and had its fireplace in an angle opposite the window. The doorway was also noticeable as a good, restrained example of early eighteenth-century work. The Lord Dysart who occupied this house as a tenant of the Duke of Norfolk was the eccentric seventh Earl, who lived here with only a man and his wife to wait on him, and who is said to have taken the place as being in proximity to the Law Courts. He was as litigious as he was eccentric, and his lawyer, who occupied a house close by (also rented by the Earl), was in constant request by his noble client. The interior of No. 12 was dirty and uncared for, and at Lord Dysart's death was found hanging with cobwebs and covered in dust. In 1893 the house was pulled down when the new red-brick buildings on the Norfolk estate were about to be erected.

In the background is the Norfolk Hotel, in Surrey Street, and the cross-thoroughfare leading to it is Howard Street. Without such aids to the topography of this picture it might be difficult nowadays for anyone to realize where they exactly were, so altered by rebuilding has now become all this quarter. The hoarding on the right indicates the demolition of old houses, the rebuilding of which is shown to be in progress in a pen-and-ink drawing of this spot taken in 1893. The structure known as Hastings House now occupies this spot.

It may not be remembered that when the Law Courts were projected a site here between Howard Street and the river was one of those suggested. Street, the architect, however, gave cogent reasons for preferring the one in the Strand which his building now occupies.

The next picture by Crowther, entitled "Old Square, Surrey Street, Strand," which was executed in 1883, presents some difficulty. What was this "Old Square," and where was it? None of the earlier writers on this part of London refers to it; and when making special

investigations about the street and the history and general topography
of this quarter for my *Annals of the Strand*, I confess to have found
nothing about it. In fact, I may as well say at once that before seeing the
title which Crowther put to this drawing I did not know of the existence of
such a feature. In none of the old plans of London, showing Surrey
Street, is there the least indication of anything but a straight narrow
street running from the Strand directly to the water's edge, with Howard
Street debouching from it on the east side and two small alleys leading
into it on the west. Parenthetically I may remark that the more northerly
of these passages was a back-way from the Strand, in which stood the
Talbot Inn (marked by Rocque), and entered Surrey Street next to a
house then numbered 35; while the lower one communicated by some
steps with Strand Lane, having its Surrey Street entrance between
Nos. 30 and 31 in that thoroughfare. It is plainly shown in Horwood's
plan, and it no doubt ran through what had been the boundary wall,
on the west, of old Arundel House gardens.

To return to Old Square, the fact is it was so called simply because
the houses here formed a square block; and had nothing to do with a
square as we generally understand the term.

The tavern shown in Crowther's drawing was the old Cheshire
Cheese, which stood at the corner of Surrey Street and Howard Street,
and had its principal front and entrance, as we here see it, in the former
thoroughfare. Almost immediately opposite to it, and therefore on the
right of, and outside, the picture, was the Norfolk Hotel; while the
turning in the background is Howard Street. In the former picture
(*vide facing Plate*) we can see the tavern's frontage to the latter thoroughfare, at the corner in the background, opposite the Norfolk Hotel. The
Cheshire Cheese has been rebuilt since those days; and I feel I must
apologize for remarking that it is not, of course, to be confounded with
the far more famous hostelry of the same name in Fleet Street.[1]

It is interesting to remember that the whole of this area, bounded
on the west by Strand Lane and on the east by Milford Lane (Agas calls
it Mylforth Lane), marks the ground on which stood Arundel House

[1] I am indebted to J. Dunn, Esq., the agent for the Norfolk estate, for illumination
on this point and others concerning this interesting locality.

LORD DYSART'S HOUSE AT THE CORNER OF
NORFOLK STREET

I

LORD DYSART'S HOUSE AT THE CORNER OF NORFOLK STREET

and its grounds which reached to the river. Agas, in his plan of 1560-70, shows Arundel House to have then been a large castellated building of far greater size and importance than any other in the neighbourhood, and even dwarfing old Somerset House. It stood about midway between the Strand and the Thames, and was flanked on the north by a range of smaller structures which no doubt formed its stables and domestic offices. Arundel Street approximately runs through the centre of the main structure. Its gardens were laid out in formal square beds, according to the fashion of the period; and in the low wall overlooking the river was a gate giving on to stairs, with a gate-house of some pretensions guarding them.

But the best views extant of this great private palace were those executed by Hollar, who lived for so long in it under the protection of the munificent Earl of Arundel. He etched many pictures of it, as well as views, from its roof, but one of the most interesting of his records is that which shows it in his remarkable bird's-eye view of the west central portion of London. There we can see, at a glance, the main structure with its chapel on the east side, its two quadrangles on the north, its great west wing stretching almost to the river bank, and Strand Lane dividing its gardens from those of Somerset House.

Before the coming of Arundel House its approximate site had been occupied by the Inn (as it was then the fashion to call such residences) of the Bishop of Bath and Wells, which had at one time been known as Hampton Place. Stow, writing at the end of the sixteenth century, speaks of this mansion as having been in his day " lately new built for a great part thereof by the Lord Thomas Seymour." I am inclined to think that some of the humbler portions (used as servants' quarters, stabling, and so forth) shown by Hollar were probably remains of the original episcopal dwelling; and it was possibly after examining this particular print that Pennant was led into his amazing statement that Arundel House was, although extensive, " low and mean " ! Such a remark is the more surprising since Pennant had only just before quoted the Duc de Sully, who was once lodged her in James I's time, as specifically stating that Arundel House was one of the finest and most extensive of the residences of the nobility in seventeenth-century London.

57

In passing through Norfolk Street I incidentally remarked that at one time William Penn lived in one of its houses. His dwelling was at the south-west corner of the thoroughfare, being actually the last house in the street, with one side of it overlooking the river. This house was numbered 21 (Horwood gives it, in his time, as No. 22), and here Penn is said to have resided, but when or for how long does not appear to be on record. According to Hawkins, in his *Life of Johnson*, " Penn chose the house as one from whence he might, on occasion, slip out by water. In the entrance to it he had a peeping hole, through which he could see any person that came to him. One of these, who had sent in his name, having been made to wait more than a reasonable time, knocked for the servant, when he asked, ' Will not thy master see me ? ' ' Friend,' answered the servant, ' he has seen thee, but he does not like thee.' The fact was that Penn had, from his station, taken a view of him and found him to be a creditor."

In the same house, at a later period, lived that Dr. Richard Brocklesby who had an equal affection for Burke and Johnson, to the former of whom he once gave £1,000, and whose benevolence to the poor whom he habitually attended without a fee, was well known in those days. He was Dr. Johnson's medical adviser, and Johnson remarks in a letter to him on the kind attention he had so long shown to his health and happiness. It seems, therefore, fairly certain that Johnson must have been a visitor to the house in Norfolk Street, and we can imagine him rolling and puffing his way down from the Strand and carefully touching each post as he passed.

It was this house of varied memories which, in course of time, became the Arundel Hotel. Crowther's picture of it is a peculiarly interesting one, as it not only shows the features of its southern frontage but also of the buildings directly to its west. Norfolk Street is seen on the right of the picture; Surrey Street on the extreme left. By the way, the entrances to the low building with the projecting window and to the large balconied house were in a little *cul-de-sac* running out of Surrey Street. Crowther made his sketch in 1881. Just eleven years before, the Embankment between Blackfriars and Westminster had been opened, and here we see what the houses on the Norfolk estate, facing it, were

THE CHESHIRE CHEESE, OLD SQUARE, SURREY STREET

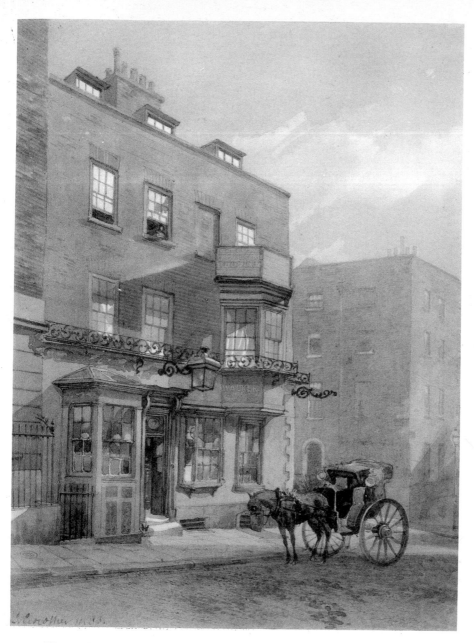

THE CHESHIRE CHEESE, OLD SQUARE, SURREY STREET

like before rebuilding on gothic lines gave them their present appearance.[1]

We must return to the Strand and proceed for a short distance east in order to study the comparative differences between the houses and shops on the south side as Crowther shows them (*vide Plate*) and as they are to-day. As a matter of fact, there are still some of the relics left here and thus the appearance of the thoroughfare on this side is not so markedly changed; although opposite, where the Law Courts now are, everything that was old has been obliterated.

The interesting old frontages which the artist depicts run from No. 217 on the right of the picture to No. 230 on its extreme left. The drawing was made in 1882, and it is curious, if we compare it with Tallis's elevation of 1838, to see how little difference there is between the two. The Bank at Nos. 217-18, next to Twining's (on the west and just outside Crowther's picture), was that of Messrs. Snow, the predecessor of Strahan, Paul and Co., whose failure created such a sensation in 1856; the original firm is said to have been started by Jeremiah Snow in 1660 at this spot, the sign of the house being then Ye Golden Anchor. As will be seen the entrance is a comparatively modern one, and the upper part has been also modernized, forming a marked antithesis to the group of old houses on its east, three of which have a tiled roof in common; while No. 220 (next the Bank) possesses a conically shaped wooden structure, a feature by the way clearly indicated in Tallis's view. Between Nos. 222 and 223 ran little Palsgrave Place, the entrance to which may be discerned next to the awning and opposite the lamp-post. Hatton, in 1708, calls this tiny byway "a pretty, spacious court, in form a parallelogram . . . a thoroughfare into Essex Court in the Temple." At one time it was called Palsgrave's Head Court, and a tavern with that sign stood at its Strand entrance; at the opposite corner the famous engraver Faithorne once lived. It was to this court that Archbishop Sanscroft fled for shelter in 1691, remaining here for some six weeks until he could safely get away to his country house in Suffolk. No. 226, nearly opposite which the old growler is standing, was in early Victorian days the Temple Bar Tea Rooms. There is nothing specially notable about the archi-

[1] The present Norfolk Hotel is in Surrey Street, and in London guides for 1818 and 1827 it is also given as being in that thoroughfare.

tectural features of these houses, but their age and variety (the curious overhanging upper part of No. 230 still remains intact) give them that picturesque air which the artist in Crowther at once realized, and he has produced in this picture a characteristic bit of the old Strand, at a spot where all around vast alterations have taken place.

When this view was taken Street's gothic building was still something of a novelty—at least to those who remembered the thoroughfare under its older and very different conditions: when Temple Bar still stood where the ridiculous Griffin now divides the traffic, and very old people could still dimly recollect Butcher's Row.

Temple Bar, which had been set up in 1672, from Wren's designs, was removed in the winter of 1878-9; and after its stones had lain derelict for some ten years they were purchased by Sir Henry Meux and re-erected as an entrance to his seat, Theobalds Park, Waltham Cross. When the Sovereign visits the City in state it is still the custom for the Lord Mayor to receive the royal cortège close to the Griffin and to hand and receive back the keys of the City. In earlier days, however, when Temple Bar was still standing here, a more decorative ceremony took place. The gates were closed, and on the arrival of the royal party a herald sounded his trumpet to indicate the fact, while another knocked and demanded entrance. Thereupon a sort of parley took place, the gates were thrown open, and the Lord Mayor appeared bearing the City sword, which he handed to the monarch, who touched it and returned it. This ceremony, which used to be observed in the time of Queen Victoria, had taken place, as Stow tells us, in that of Elizabeth; although the Temple Bar of those days was a very different structure from that which Wren designed.

It is practically on this site that Crowther made his picture. The Griffin was unveiled in September 1880 by the late Duke of Albany. The dragon itself was designed by C. B. Birch, A.R.A., and the figures of Queen Victoria and Edward Prince of Wales were the work of Sir Edgar Boehm. The portrait of the Lord Mayor introduced is that of Sir Francis Truscott. The architect of the whole thing was Sir Horace Jones.

When the statue was first erected the medallion reliefs were of stone,

THE ARUNDEL HOTEL, ARUNDEL STREET

Embankment Front

THE ARUNDEL HOTEL, ARUNDEL STREET

Embankment Front

THE STRAND, OPPOSITE THE LAW COURTS

but mischievous people broke off the little heads, and they were therefore
replaced by bronze ones. The laſt of them, representing Queen Victoria
going to the Guildhall in 1837, was not inserted till 1882.

It is indeed at this point in the Strand, where it so soon merges into
Fleet Street, that the architectural changes which succeeding periods
have brought in their train are moſt marked. For not only has the great
Aldwych-Kingsway development altered the alignment of the thoroughfare out of all recognition, but that scheme shouldered out of exiſtence
two of the ſtreets which were notable as being survivals of a time when
London had not become grandiose and was ſtill picturesque.

But in addition to this, in the earlier part of the nineteenth century,
to be precise in 1813, Butcher's Row, which rather further eaſt had
impinged on the roadway much as Holywell Street did till our own time,
had been removed, and that portion of the Strand thus widened by its
disappearance became known as Pickett Street. In course of time this
section of the thoroughfare was obliterated by the erection of the Law
Courts, which were begun in 1874, and opened some half a dozen years
later. It is unnecessary to enlarge on the by-ſtreets, such as Serle Street,
Little Shire Lane, Newcaſtle Court, Boswell's Court, and the reſt which
the coming of Street's gothic pile wiped out of exiſtence; the holocauſt
can be matched by the truncation of Clement's Inn, the disappearance of
Lyon's Inn and New Inn, and their adjoining byways, due to the formation of Aldwych and Kingsway.

But it will be observed that there have been many successive rehabili-
tations of the thoroughfare at this point during something over the laſt
century, and now there is little, one may almoſt generalize with safety
and say nothing, left here linking our days with those of the earlier
Georges except the few old houses we have been examining, and the two
churches which seem like a couple of galleons sailing weſtward through
the ſtill relatively narrow " ſtraits of the Strand," as a portion of the ſtreet
juſt eaſt of St. Clement's Danes was once actually called. Those two
dear, dirty, delightful ſtreets, of which Crowther has left us pictures,
Holywell and Wych Streets, possessed something of the fascination which
attaches to decorative old age. Many of us can ſtill well remember
them, with their overhanging firſt floors, their grimy windows, their

signs (at least one sign remained) and, in the former, the congregated bookshops.

How often has one not loitered in Booksellers' Row, and hunted for, and sometimes secured, bargains. There was Denny's, with its new books, at the west end, just behind St. Mary's Church, and there was Ridler's, with its ancient tomes tucked away in a corner at the east end; while between them on each hand were the alluring bibliographical wares of others, spread out in a dual attraction, and making it necessary continually to tack across the little lane. For it was nothing but a lane, and although it possessed a roadway, suitable for the passage of sedan chairs, I never myself happen to have seen a " hansom " or a " growler " in it. Indeed, it was made for walking in; and that it should have disappeared before the incidence of the taxi is among the fitting things of life. A taxi in Holywell Street! One would as soon have expected to see a megalosaurus in the Strand itself. Those who do not remember Holywell Street and Wych Street cannot quite know the London of the nineteenth century; cannot quite visualize what it must have looked like a century before. What they know is a new and stone-built city towering away to the skies, where it is difficult to take breath for a moment amid the turmoil of the rushing, headlong London of to-day.

And so it is that we like, even the most modern of us on occasion, to recapture something of the old air, in the pictures in which such diligent and accurate draughtsmen as Crowther have been at pains to set down the picturesqueness which is gradually eluding us as we wander about the streets. For except where the trees and the grass have been left with their essential gift of beauty, and here and there, some bit of warm brick-work which, by the grace of God and a ground landlord, has not been captured and devoured by the moloch of bricks and mortar, London is fast losing all claim to that charm which it once possessed. Everything is now on a vast scale; a building megalomania has set in, and for much that is dignified, something that is even beautiful, we have more that is frankly vulgar and ostentatious; and when you see a new building blotting out the sky and scraping the very stars, one's first thought is not who designed it, not its architectural lines, but amazement at what it must have cost.

And as the cost of London has increased, so its value has lessened—not its rateable value, not its intrinsic worth in so much building material and florid decoration, but its value as an aesthetic entity; its value as an influence and an inspiration. . . .

But, as you justly remark, these memories of the past are carrying us far away from the Strand, and it is the Strand in one of its most picturesque manifestations with which Crowther is concerned in two of his pictures. It is convenient to take No. 33 first, not only because in the old days this end of Holywell and Wych Streets was just opposite the Arundel Street about whose purlieus we have been wandering, but also because we are now on our way back to Waterloo Bridge, and so should properly begin at the furthermost point east in Holywell Street, the left-hand thoroughfare facing us in Crowther's drawing.

In the later 'eighties, and indeed till the demolition of the block, the shop at the north-east corner was Hill's, the second-hand bookseller's (I have a little book now—*Manon Lescaut*—which I bought there then); in the picture, which was executed in 1881, the premises appear to be those of a printseller's (if I am correct in making out the name over the window) called Albert Wilson. The twin building at the south-east corner of Wych Street was a public-house—The Rising Sun. At a later date the front of this tavern was altered, the window being converted into an entrance with double swing-doors, and the narrow inlet shown in Crowther's picture being made into a window; a large hanging lamp in front was also added. A little way up Wych Street and nearly opposite The Rising Sun was the entrance to Dane's Inn, and a little further west the fronts of the houses forming part of New Inn. The former occupied the site of the more ancient Angel Inn, and was not an Inn of Chancery, having been merely a collocation of chambers available for anyone who chose to pay for them. New Inn, on the other hand, belonged to the Middle Temple, to which it formed a sort of annexe. So early as the reign of Edward IV we hear of Sir John Fineux, Chief Justice of the King's Bench, leasing it for the use of law students. The one notable man we can now connect with it in such a capacity was Sir Thomas More, who was a member before he joined Lincoln's Inn.

Nearly opposite, and situated between Wych Street and Holywell

Street, was Lyon's Inn. Like Dane's Inn it was originally an ordinary hostelry, but in Henry VIII's reign was converted into an Inn of Chancery. It has a long and interesting history;[1] but eventually the Law quitted it, and it was let out in chambers in which Captain Costigan and the Chevalier Strong, as well as Mr. Weare, whom Thurtell murdered, had their habitats; so that many ghosts were put to rout when the place was demolished in 1863.

But, after all, Wych Street, really older than Holywell Street as it was, had not in our day quite the same glamour about it; although, as we can see from the frontispiece to this volume, its old houses were every whit as effective as those in the twin street. For one thing it was less of a thoroughfare for pedestrians; and the street that had once been a kind of continuation of Drury Lane had come to be little more than a back lane, interesting to the antiquary on account of its architectural survivals, but not specially alluring to the mere man, and especially, inasmuch as booksellers did not affect it, the book-man. Nos. 34 and 35 were good examples of the attractive old houses that were to be seen here, and they stood on the south side nearly opposite the entrance into New Inn. The whole street had in its ultimate days become very shabby and dirty, and no little of its architectural charm was stultified in consequence. The Rising Sun, as I have mentioned, was a feature in it; while an earlier one, The Shakespeare's Head, No. 31, had had for its landlord for a number of years no less Falstaffian a personage, in manners as well as appearance, than the famous Mark Lemon, once editor of *Punch*. This fact resulted in The Shakespeare's Head becoming a recognized resort for literary men and wits, and Dickens and Douglas Jerrold were among its frequent habitués.

Another inn, The Angel, here, at a still earlier period, was the scene of an historic event, for from it, in 1554, Bishop Hooper was taken away to be martyred at Gloucester. One of the old gabled houses on the south side was sometimes known as that of Jack Sheppard, who was much associated with all this part, and may very well have inhabited it or robbed those who did.

---

[1] See for an account of it, and other Inns of Chancery in this neighbourhood, the author's *Annals of the Strand*.

EAST END OF HOLYWELL STREET
AND WYCH STREET

K

EAST END OF HOLYWELL STREET
AND WYCH STREET

There were entrances from Wych Street to three of the tiny little theatres which, in these days, would go so short a way in providing for audiences swelled to mammoth dimensions. One of these playhouses was the Olympic, which occupied the site of the once famous and historic Craven House, once the temporary abode of the unfortunate Queen of Bohemia, to whom her devoted admirer, Lord Craven, the hero of Kreuznach, had lent it.

Astley built the Olympic, and opened it in 1806. After carrying it on for six years he sold it to Elliston, and on its boards appeared at later dates such well-known histrions as Benjamin Webster, Ada Cavendish, who married Frank Marshall and made a hit as Mercy Merrick in " The New Magdalen," and Henry Neville.

Another little theatre, The Globe, built on a portion of the site of Lyon's Inn, had one of its entrances in Wych Street. It was constructed in a hole made originally for the foundations of a projected hotel, so that the dress circle was on the ground level, the stage and pit being, of course, below. It was opened in 1868, and here " Les Cloches de Corneville " and " Our Boys " had phenomenal successes as had, later, " The Private Secretary " and the still evergreen " Charley's Aunt "; while it was here that, still earlier, Jennie Lee scored such a triumph with her impersonation of " Jo " in the dramatized version of *Bleak House*—curiously enough, close to some of Joe's distressful haunts.

The other playhouse which had a connection with Wych Street, inasmuch as the stage was reached by a long flight of stairs from that thoroughfare, was The Opéra Comique, the principal entrance of which was in the Strand by an underground passage beneath Holywell Street. It was opened two years after The Globe, and was chiefly identified with French plays, *opéra bouffe*, vaudeville, and so forth. One remembers all these little places; but to write about them sounds, as it is, alas! like writing ancient history.

Of all the pictures (and there are many) of Holywell Street with which I am acquainted this one by Crowther is, I think, the most effective, and the most truthful. For it not only reproduces the quaintest of its old houses, but it gives a singularly accurate idea of the dimensions of the thoroughfare. Taking it in conjunction with Dr. Philip Norman's beautiful version (which shows us the street looking east) we have a complete idea of its outlines, its intrinsic (though I am bound to say dirty) beauty, and its unforgettable charm. In it the " unimaginable touch of time " had, indeed, produced something almost unique in the London of our earlier days. Of no special historical interest Holywell Street had yet come to wear its garb of antiquity with something of the distinguished air of a tragedian whose day is over, but who cannot forget his large and dignified past. It was a survival which should have been cherished. But sentiment is nowhere when building development is abroad, and Holywell Street is as much forgotten as Tadmor. To realize its site even, you must superimpose a plan of what London is to-day over what it was when Dr. Johnson puffed his way down this exiguous thoroughfare, even over what it was in the memory of those who would resent the accusation of being as yet old.

It took its name, of course, from the spring where, on Holy Thursdays, the Ascension was solemnly commemorated and newly baptized converts appeared in their white robes; where, too, the Canterbury Pilgrims had one of their halting places—the time when all this part was open country, and the few houses shown in Wyngaerde's map had not come into existence. In Elizabeth's day the nucleus of the street was formed; and by the eighteenth century it was inhabited, as Strype tells us, " by divers salesmen and piece-workers." On May days, when the Maypole, at its east end, was decorated, and festivities took place, the street must have been seen at its best.

Crowther's picture, besides giving an excellent general idea, accentuates one special feature here—the sign of the Half Moon with a human face (really but the first quarter)[1] which hung over No. 36, on the left hand of the picture (it was one of the last surviving signs in London), and was opposite Half Moon Passage, the little entrance to Lyon's Inn. There can be seen the entrance to another alley on this side of No. 36; Horwood does not show this in his plan, but it was a narrow passage

[1] According to Diprose, it was the sign of a staymaker patronized by the Royal Family in the time of George III. Later the shop was occupied by a mercer, whose bill-heads bore this sign. It afterwards became a bookseller's.

66

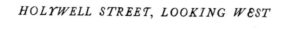

HOLYWELL STREET, LOOKING WEST

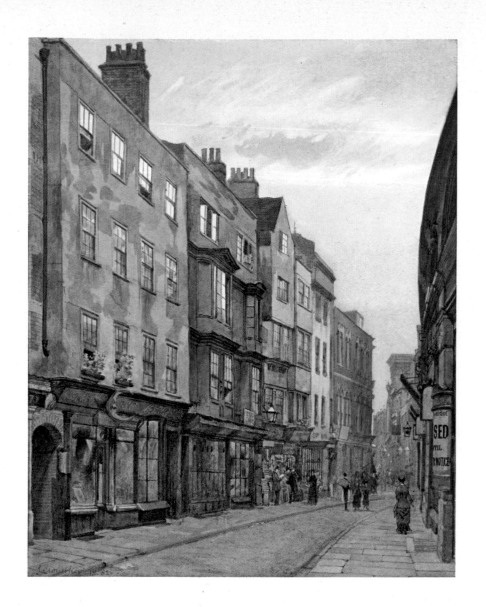

leading into the Strand. At one time there was another sign of a lion, grotesquely formed (probably associated with Lyon's Inn), at the corner of a house also on the south side of the street, and this remained till the 'nineties, when it was removed, and is now in the Guildhall Museum.

CHAPTER V

THE BOROUGH, SOUTHWARK

IN order to reach the other side of the river, where Crowther made so many interesting water-colour drawings, a number of which are here reproduced, it will be convenient to retrace our steps to Waterloo Bridge; for one thing because that is our nearest approach to the south bank, and particularly because the artist has left us a picture of it.

Waterloo Bridge, the ultimate fate of which is still in the balance, has become in recent days more talked about than any monument in London. Everyone is aware of the critical state of that remarkable achievement; many people are, probably for the first time, coming to realize its essential beauty. The Londoner generally requires the destruction of a monument or a threat to destroy it before he seems to consider it an artistic as well as a utilitarian possession. Waterloo Bridge has been a marked instance of this, and as a result of much advertising of the fact that the structure is one to be proud of, we have all become proud of it; and it is safe to say that for one who admired its beauty of line, its dignity, its curiously happy blending with Somerset House (London's finest building), a thousand recognized in it nothing but a highway from one bank of the Thames to the other. It seems almost superfluous to remind the reader that it was built in pursuance of an Act passed in 1809, that its first stone was laid on 11th October 1811, and that it was opened by the Prince Regent on 18th June 1817. It is the supreme achievement of John Rennie, and so imposing was it found, at least by foreigners, that one, Canova, affirmed it to be one of the features of the city that chiefly struck him, and another, M. Dupin, asserted that it was " a colossal monument worthy of Sesostris and the Cæsars."

Some time since, when writing about the bridge, I had an opportunity of reading Rennie's MS. account of its initiation and progress. Much of this interesting matter is, of course, technical, and would prove

WATERLOO BRIDGE FROM CHARING CROSS RAILWAY BRIDGE

OLD WOODEN HOUSES IN ROYAL MINT STREET

OLD WOODEN HOUSES IN ROYAL MINT STREET

tiresome if not unintelligible to the lay mind; but I may record here that the total cost of the bridge itself was but £565,000; the making of the approaches and the necessary acquisition of land and buildings, etc., amounting to a further £485,000. It was due to the speculation of a private company, and was far from a successful one. In 1877 the Metropolitan Board of Works purchased the structure for £475,000, and on the 5th October of the following year it was made free of tolls.

It is not generally known (as the saying is) that the treadle and index at the toll-houses, a most ingenious contrivance for rendering fraud impossible, were invented by Mr. Lethbridge, the property-man at Drury Lane Theatre.

The first person to pass across the bridge was, appropriately, the Duke of Wellington, who duly paid his penny. There is a point about it (by the way, it was for a short time called the Strand Bridge) which is often overlooked. It was in the nature of a national memorial (a utilitarian one, but none the less significant for that) to those who had fought against Napoleon and had ensured the safety of this country from foreign domination. As such it has something in common with the Cenotaph, which we are all proud to salute in Whitehall. That deeply significant monument stands as a permanent remembrance of those who gave their lives for the country in a struggle immeasurably more tremendous, but in many respects similar to that which took place a century earlier on the battle-ground of Europe. Apart from all other considerations of use and necessity, Waterloo Bridge should surely be preserved on this ground alone, that it typifies that devotion to the country which in its hour of need kept it intact from " foreign levy." What should we say if, a hundred years later, a suggestion was made to destroy the Cenotaph, which has been, in our own time, raised amid the grief of myriads, because it was in the way of the traffic; or because it had become dangerous and some of our descendants chose to assert that it was past repair?

As a matter of fact, Waterloo Bridge has one serious drawback in these days. It is too narrow. When it was constructed no one could have had the least idea of the increase in traffic, or the size and weight of the vehicles which have, in relatively recent times, been placed on our long-suffering roads. Consequently it is condemned for what its conſtructor could not possibly have foreseen. What would seem a solution to the difficulty would be the building of a bridge at Charing Cross adequate for present needs in this respect and the reſtoration of Waterloo Bridge to pedeſtrian and perhaps light traffic—cabs and carriages and so forth. With this and the removal of Charing Cross Station to the south bank, as well as the formation of an embankment on that side of the river, the traffic problem would be capable of solution in a way that otherwise appears to be impossible.

But this is by the way, and I muſt say a few words about Crowther's view of Waterloo Bridge, especially as it seems quite as likely as not that that beautiful ſtructure may be sacrificed to an *idée fixe* which seems to see in its deſtruction the only way out of a vehicular imbroglio. The artiſt, as we see, has chosen the weſt side of the bridge from which to take its picture. By doing this he selected the moſt imposing view. For not only do we thus get Somerset House flanking Rennie's remarkable ſtructure, but we have it and its attendant church ſteeple balanced on the south bank by the Shot Tower which, were it in Bologna or St. Gimigiano, would be gazed at as an artiſtic object, but as it is only in London is regarded as a mere chimney-ſtack, merely worthy to be adorned by the flamboyant advertisements of commerce. But chiefly was Crowther right in his choice of this side of the bridge, because he is thus able to concentrate on the noble dome of St. Paul's, the cumulation of all London's buildings, towering up in the centre of the picture and adding to the dignity of Waterloo Bridge its own inalienable dignity. As we look at this view we are gazing at the heart of the empire, to which so many features lend symbolical significance. Commerce is here, and the seat of officialdom; here, too, is the fineſt of the links binding up the two Londons, that of the north and that of the south bank; while in the diſtance rises the architectural maſterpiece typifying something greater and more enduring than all—the emblem of the hopes and fears and beliefs of a great nation.

The drawings, which have been selected from those Crowther made of intereſting landmarks on the south side of the river, range from spots in the Borough, through Bermondsey and Southwark, to Lambeth, Stockwell, and Battersea. The area is one which, owing largely to the

THE WHITE HART INN, BOROUGH

THE WHITE HART INN, BOROUGH

absence of an embankment on the Surrey shore, is somewhat of a *terra incognita* to most people. It has, in the course of time, been overbuilt with small houses, and in consequence the fine old mansions which in former days stood there in a rural environment, have gradually disappeared. Long noted for its inns, which existed on the then outskirts of the city as the early stages in the journeyings of the pilgrims of old, and later in those of more sophisticated travellers, it has become a rather derelict area whence the remains of past times have long since gone the way of all bricks and mortar; and anyone penetrating into its purlieus will have difficulty in reconstructing those earlier days when picturesque taverns and even great mansions dotted it, and it was alive with the goings and comings of the Canterbury Pilgrims of one age or the Pickwick Pilgrims of another. Nowadays we see the tops of its dreary dwellings from a railway carriage as it bears us away to the Sussex Downs or the Weald of Kent, or is the first stage in those longer excursions which have their objective in continental centres.

Indeed, except for the purposes of business or for those who live in these parts, the south side of the river is cut off from the citizen in a quite surprising way. You go to London Bridge or Waterloo Stations with a definite object, and as your car or taxi hurries you through the trifling distance between these termini and the bridges, you not unwillingly close your eyes to the dirt and squalor that exhibit themselves within a quarter of a mile of London's centre. It is a matter of amazement to those who trouble themselves to think about it that this should be so, and that we have so willingly, as it were, disregarded our opportunities as to neglect the development of this large area which lies at our very doors, and have been so long content that our great and splendid river should be the one-sided stream it is. Years ago an embankment on the south side similar to that on the north ought to have been constructed. Had this been done, a gradual betterment of the area between Westminster and London Bridges would have resulted, and it is probable that the traffic problem (about which we are all busying ourselves) would never have arisen, at least in the acute form in which it to-day manifests itself.

When the London County Council erected its immense palace one thought that perhaps here would be a beginning to supply this crying need; but not so. As if a settled determination on the part of the authorities had been arrived at to stop once and for ever an embankment, the building was placed so close to the Thames that a roadway cannot now be run between it and the river; and thus if one ever does come anywhere on the south side, it is for all time prevented from being continuous from Waterloo Bridge to Westminster Bridge—until the County Hall is pulled down.

In the remote future then all this vast area may become improved, but it will apparently be in that far-off day when Macaulay's New Zealander is musing over the ruins of old London and improvising plans for a new one.

If we pass over the Waterloo Bridge of Crowther's drawing, to-day heavily leaning on its crutches, and with the engineering doctors disputing as to the possibility of its rehabilitation, and all the world wondering as to its probability, we shall find ourselves in that region known as The Borough, the centre of which may be placed at St. George's Circus. All this area was once known as St. George's Fields, where, by the way, Falstaff and Shallow once " lay all night in the windmill," and where people used to congregate for all sorts of purposes ranging from the riotry connected with Lord George Gordon's propaganda to the attentive congregations listening to John Wesley's eloquence. But this is to go back far beyond the day when, as James Smith writes in *The Rejected Addresses*:

> Saint George's fields are fields no more;
> The trowel supersedes the plough;
> Swamps, huge and inundate of yore,
> Are changed to civic villas now.

One of its most interesting thoroughfares was that known as Mint Street, perpetuating by its name the Mint which, originally a centre for the official manufacture of coinage, passed, in process of time, to a place of sanctuary for those who were not specially identified with its uses, and as a harbour for such as were notable for its abuses; in a word, insolvent people congregated here together with thieves and other lawless members of the community.

72

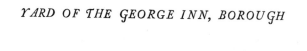

YARD OF THE GEORGE INN, BOROUGH

YARD OF THE GEORGE INN, BOROUGH

THE KING'S HEAD INN, BOROUGH

According to Strype, " The Mint generally so taken is very large, containing several streets and alleys; and in this tract of ground called the Mint stood the Duke of Suffolk's house." " The chief street in the Mint (Mint Street)," he adds, " is so-called, being that which gives an entrance into it out of Blackman Street "; while Stow remarks that "a Mint of Coinage was there kept for the King." The whole region was one not very dissimilar from the better known Alsatia off Fleet Street, and in the eighteenth century people like Nat. Lee and Nahum Tate, the Poet Laureate, were inhabitants for a time of a region which excited the irony of Young and the satire of Pope.

" The man of rhyme," whom the latter visualizes as walking forth from the Mint to waylay the poet " just at dinner time," had many an actual prototype; while such people as " Mat of the Mint," one of Macheath's gang mentioned in *The Beggar's Opera*, were to be found here in an abundance that speaks volumes for the essentially vicious character of the place. Having established by a sort of unwritten law their right to asylum in this area, the inhabitants evolved, in process of time, certain customs and privileges of which, in many instances, it would have been hard to trace the origin. Thus we are told that should a bailiff have ventured to enter this territory, he was liable to be seized and searched for proof of his office; this found, he was incontinently dragged to a pump and there received a thorough drenching; this was followed by a ducking in a sewer; and finally he was forced to kiss a brickbat that had been lavishly immersed in filth, and to swear that he would never repeat the heinous offence of doing what his calling required. He was likewise mulcted in whatever he had in his pockets in order that gin might be purchased with the proceeds, and if he was found to be without this means of paying his footing he was again ducked and treated with further indignities. The officers of the law had no sinecure in those lawless, spacious days!

Although such immunities as appear to have been first afforded the Mint in the days of William III were finally abolished in those of the later Georges, the place still retained for many a long year after its distinctively dirty and demoralized character; and at the risk of being tedious I venture to quote a description of it, as it was in 1852, when the writer, Thomas Miller, published his *Picturesque Sketches of London*, in which the passage appears:

"Stretching from St. George's Church, in the Borough," he says, "into the high road which leads to the cast-iron bridge[1] of Southwark, are no end of narrow courts, winding alleys, and ruined houses, which a bold-hearted man would hesitate to thread after dusk. Here stand numbers of houses which are unroofed and uninhabited. Years ago they were doomed to be pulled down, and it was resolved that a wide, open street should be built upon the space they now occupy: years may still roll away before they are removed. There is no place like this in the suburbs of London—no spot that looks so murderous, so melancholy, and so miserable. Many of these houses, besides being old, are very large and lofty. Many of these courts stand just as they did when Cromwell sent out his spies to hunt up and slay the Cavaliers, just as they again were hunted in return, after the Restoration, by the Royalists, who threaded their intricacies, with sword and pistol in hand, in search of the fallen Roundheads. There is a smell of past ages about these ancient courts, like that which arises from decay—a murky closeness—as if the old winds which blew through them in the time of the civil wars had become stagnant, and all old things had fallen and died just as they were blown together and left to perish. So it is now. The timber of these old houses looks bleached and dead; and the very brickwork seems never to have been new. In them you find wide, hollow-sounding, decayed staircases that lead into great ruinous rooms, whose echoes are only awakened by the shrieking and running of large black-eyed rats, which eat through the solid floors, through the wainscot, and live and die without being startled by a human voice. From the Southwark Bridge Road you may see the roofs of many of these great desolate houses; they are broken and open; and the mossy oaken rafters are exposed to the summer sun and the snow of winter. Some of the lower floors are still inhabited; and at the end of these courts you will see standing, on a fine day, such characters as you will meet with nowhere beside in the neighbourhood of London. Their very dress is peculiar;

[1] This was designed by Rennie, and was opened in 1819. A new bridge, from the plans of the late Sir Ernest George, has in recent years taken its place.

THE YARD OF THE QUEEN'S HEAD INN, BOROUGH

and they frequent the dark and hidden public-houses which abound in these close alleys—places where the gas is burning all day long. Excepting the courts behind Long-lane, in Smithfield, we know no spot in London like this, which yet fronts St. George's Church, in the Borough."

This description, although published in 1852, had been written seven years earlier, and during the ensuing half-century great changes had taken place. But as if nothing was capable of making this area clean and personable, it still remains with a certain atmosphere of dreariness upon it, and the imagination has no little difficulty in clearing away these successive layers of building development which arose on the green fields where the bull- and bear-baiting rings once drew crowds, and the famous theatres with which the immortal name of Shakespeare is for all time identified.

There is a picture extant showing Mint Street as it was in 1825, with the old houses and their vast overhanging eaves, in some cases their semi-octagonal windows (perhaps relics of the Duke of Suffolk's palace), and ancient timbers of a remote past. This was the part that Dickens as a boy knew, and here, in Lant Street, which takes its name from the ground landlord's, he places Bob Sawyer and Robert Allan. Unfortunately the old houses of a century ago had long since disappeared when Crowther was scouring this portion of the city for features worthy to be perpetuated because of their associations or their intrinsic architectural beauties. But curiously enough he has left us a water-colour of the other Mint Street (Royal Mint Street it should properly be called) close to the Tower; and although this is not in our regular itinerary, no one, I think, will object to its being reproduced here. In fact, so changed are both these thoroughfares that I might have included it as the Southwark Mint Street itself, and few would have probably been any the wiser. As I do venture to include it, I shall naturally be expected to say something about this far-flung thoroughfare. Royal Mint Street may not convey much to the reader, but as Rosemary Lane and Rag Fair it enters into history as well as literature. By these names, indeed, it was known indifferently till 1850 when it was rechristened more appropriately, since it runs behind the spot where the coins of the realm are manufactured. Although its houses may have changed, its earlier customs survive, and there are as many (probably more) old clothes shops in it

75

than there were when their presence gave it its alternative title, and the " tattered ensigns of Rag Fair " became immortalized in *The Dunciad*. " There is no expressing the poverty of the goods; nor yet their cheapness," said Pennant in 1790; and in 1926 we might re-echo the remark. But to-day you will find it hard to discover a " pincushion-maker," such as Goldsmith speaks of, there; and no Captain Jack of Defoe's imaginative actuality haunts the place. Indeed, if ghosts walk the one that should haunt it uneasily on every 30th January is that of Richard Brandon who died here, and who is said to have been the man who cut off Charles I's head. How this could have been, however, it is difficult to imagine, as in the burial registry of St. Mary's, Whitechapel, is the entry: " 1646, June 21st Rich. Brandon, a man out of Rosemary Lane "; so if this date is correct he must have come to life again to do his regicidal act a year and a half later!

The old wooden houses shown in Crowther's drawing were numbered 2 to 4 Royal Mint Street, and together with red brick ones beyond gave a touch of picturesqueness to the thoroughfare which only old clothes can (if they can) now give.

It was in Southwark, to which we return from this wandering, that some of the most notable of London's old taverns congregated, first stages many of them in the journeyings of merchants and pilgrimages to Becket's shrine. Among them was the Hart, as Stow concisely terms it. This was none other than the famous White Hart, at what in time became No. 61 Borough High Street, which was in all probability the largest of these caravanserais at which so many travellers stopped for rest and refreshment. It no doubt dated from the latter part of the fourteenth century, as its sign was the badge of Richard II. We know, on the authority of Hall's Chronicle and the Paston Letters, that Jack Cade made it his head-quarters, and there caused an unfortunate enemy named " Hawaydyne, of St. Martyn's," to be put to death. After thus entering indirectly into the annals of the country the White Hart rested in obscurity, on its laurels, for a long period. In 1529 it emerges as a suggested meeting-place with Thomas Cromwell, on the part of one who desired an interview with that redoubtable minister; and Taylor, the water poet, strings its name into one of his verses.

76

BACK VIEW OF THE QUEEN'S HEAD INN, BOROUGH

BACK VIEW OF THE QUEEN'S HEAD INN, BOROUGH

In 1669 it was partially destroyed by fire—a fire so considerable that the landlord, one Geary, is said to have " undone " himself by spending the then large sum of £700 in rebuilding. But a worse fate was in store for the place, for just seven years later the great fire of Southwark entirely gutted it. And again Geary rebuilt it. This time the cost was so great, no less, indeed, than £2,400, that the indomitable tenant was only able to meet it by the aid of friends. The tavern was at that time owned by one John Collett, and as a set-forth to Geary's expenditure he gave him a further lease of sixty years at a rent of £55.

Thence onward the White Hart began a new life as one of the largest and most patronized inns in the vicinity, as Strype, in 1720, indicates it as then being.

But all earlier incidents connected with it have become merged in the outstanding fact that Dickens immortalized it in the pages of Pickwick. The novelist's description of the place, as well as Phiz's well-known picture of its courtyard, with Sam Weller cleaning innumerable pairs of boots, and Mr. Pickwick and Mr. Perker asking him leading questions, are familiar to everyone. It is a tremendous thought that had there been no White Hart Sam might never have entered Pickwick's service and, of course, the immortal middle-class epic—perhaps the best known book in the world, after the Bible—need, for all practical purposes, never have been written!

Down to 1866 the old tavern remained essentially as it had been since the 1676 rebuilding, but in that year a portion of it which had probably become decayed was rebuilt, and a new side to the courtyard, on the south, was erected. Still the old galleries existed on the other three sides of the yard as they did down to 1889, just ten years after Crowther made his beautiful picture of the structure, when the tavern was demolished.

But this yard had not been entirely unspoilt in other respects, for in the 'seventies of the nineteenth century a certain Spencer, a bacon-curer, was allowed to erect an unsightly pent-house which rose sufficiently to hide the lower tier of gallery rails; and the upper portion had been let out in tenements, the business of the house being carried on in the rebuilt portion. There was also an inner and larger yard, and that part of the old structure which looked out on it was also let to lodgers.

Dr. Philip Norman, whose knowledge of London is unrivalled, and who, unlike most topographers, possesses the art of making beautiful pictures to accompany his written descriptions, has preserved, in several of the former, the appearance of the White Hart as it was in 1884,[1] and these may be compared with that which Crowther produced five years earlier.

Just ten years after this view of the old inn was taken it was pulled down and offices were erected on its site. If we examine Crowther's drawing we shall have a good idea of what the general appearance of these old galleried yards were like. Unfortunately, when the picture was executed modern rebuilding had to some extent stultified the general picturesqueness of that of the White Hart, and on the right can be seen painful evidence of this; while the row of sheds on the left has almost entirely hidden the lower balcony. The place, as I have said, had been for long let out in tenements, and the business of the house was carried on in the new-built premises which bore, as we see, on their Victorian front built in 1865-6, the somewhat misleading legend: " The Old White Hart." Through the archway can be seen the inner yard. In 1884 the stabling had been pulled down, but some curious old houses remained which, at that time, were crowded with tenants; and in the main portion (that backing on the part shown in Crowther's background, under which the archway runs) a bacon-curer had his premises, and Dr. Norman speaks of the smoke from his furnace curling out of the windows! But in spite of such changes the spirit of the picturesque and antique hung about the place with its red-tiled roof and its carved oak balustrade matured by the mystic touch of time.

There has never been much doubt that Dickens, when describing the inn yard in which the momentous first interview between Mr. Pickwick and Sam Weller took place, indicated that of the White Hart; but there has been one notable dissentient from this view, and Mr. Ashby-Sterry was always firmly convinced that the novelist had in his eye, not this inn at all, but the George, which stood, and happily one can say stands (although it is to be sure sadly truncated) close by. I confess myself unable to share Mr. Ashby-Sterry's opinion on this point. I

[1] See *London, Vanished and Vanishing*, 1905.

INTERIOR OF THE WHITE LYON PRISON

M

INTERIOR OF THE WHITE LYON PRISON

wish I could for the yard of the George may yet be trodden, and a portion of its wooden gallery still overlooks it—sole survivors of what was once fairly common. The George is one of the " many fair inns " in this neighbourhood,[1] recorded by Stow as being in existence at the close of the sixteenth century. Indeed, it is spoken of as the " St. George " forty odd years before Stow wrote. As the George, *tout court*, it dates from 1558, when it belonged to Humfrey Colet, who had been Member of Parliament for Southwark, and it was at that time tenanted by one Nicholas Martin. That rebuilding had taken place in the time of Charles I is proved by a return made concerning the tavern in 1634, in which the fact is specifically mentioned that it had been reconstructed in brick and timber twelve years earlier.

It is not often that we get any personal references to the old inns in the seventeenth century, but there is one such referring to this tavern in *Musarum Deliciæ*, published in 1656, in which are some lines " upon a surfeit caught by drinking bad sack at the George Tavern, in Southwark," in which the " posset-drinke " is said to be " too bad for hereticks."

By an extant token we know that one Anthony Blake was mine host at this period, but whether or not it was he who was responsible for this indifferent cheer is not recorded. A later tenant was Mark Weyland. Inns, like theatres, seem to be curiously subject to fires, and one such during Weyland's time, in 1670, partially destroyed the George, which was destined wholly to fall a victim to the great conflagration in Southwark six years later, a fire that burnt down practically all this part of London.

Weyland's business was carried on by his widow, who was followed successively by William Golding and Thomas Green, whose niece, Mrs. Schofield, and her husband came here in 1809; the lady surviving as " hostess " till 1859.

That the George had been rebuilt soon after the last fire on much the same lines as before is evidenced by the existing remains of the characteristic galleried yard; and that it continued as a flourishing concern is

---

[1] This part was originally known as Long Southwark; the name of " the Borough " not generally being applied to it before the eighteenth century.

shown by a notice, which appeared in 1825, to the effect that it was then
" a good commercial inn—whence several coaches and many waggons
depart laden with the merchandize of the metropolis, in return for which
they bring back from various parts of Kent, etc., that staple article of the
country, the hop, to which we are indebted for the good quality of the
London porter."

In course of time the property passed into the hands of Guy's
Hospital, but later, somewhere in the 'seventies of the last century, it was
sold to the Great Northern Railway. It was then found necessary, alas!
to pull down a large portion of the old place, and this was done in 1889.
When Crowther made his drawing, however, he selected what must have
been then the most picturesque feature of it; and it is a matter of con-
gratulation for those to whom such relics are dear, that that portion still
remains much as it was these forty-five years ago. What, since the
'eighties, is new are the buildings which have replaced those shown in
the background to the right of the galleried portion. Then, too, the
entrance from the High Street was by a narrow way immediately next to
this old feature, a way down which Crowther shows a cart proceeding.
Now, this has been closed and a larger and higher entrance has been
made to its right, where the house with the large windows is shown as
then existing. That portion in the foreground on the left is now used
by the London and North Eastern Railway, and a low wooden paling
divides the pavement in front of it from the yard.

A few years ago (1918) Mr. B. W. Matz, the great Dickens authority,
wrote a little brochure on the George, illustrated by a number of photo-
graphs showing its various stages, as well as its snug bar-parlour, its
old taproom and coffee-room, and the first floor gallery of which Crowther has left us his charming picture of the exterior. In these days when
demolition is rampant anyone interested in the relatively few old relics
of the past as are permitted to remain in London, should make an
opportunity of visiting the George where the *aura* of the past still lingers
and where no one need fear the drink provided, be he never so great a
" heretick."

Just as the White Hart and the George were burnt down in 1676,
so the next tavern of which Crowther executed a picture—the King's

MARSHALSEA PRISON
A Sky-Parlour

MARSHALSEA PRISON

A Sky-Parlour

Head—shared the same fate. This tremendous fire, indeed, consumed the best part of Southwark (although the Queen's Head, to which we shall come, somehow escaped), from the Bridge to St. Margaret's Hill, the Town Hall, which had been erected in 1540, falling a victim to the flames. It broke out at about four o'clock in the morning of 26th May and continued during the whole of that day and well into the following night, before it burnt itself out. The old wooden and lath and plaster houses fell an easy prey to the flames, especially as the means of coping with fires in those days were archaic in the extreme. Everything was done, however, blowing up houses and such like drastic efforts, to limit the area of devastation. The Duke of Monmouth, the Earl of Craven, the Lord Mayor, and other notable people were present, urging on those who tried to save what was possible; even the King himself, accompanied by the Duke of York, we are told, " in the tender sense of the calamity, being pleased himself to go down to the bridge in his barge, to give such orders as his Majesty found fit for putting a stop to it, which, through the mercy of God, was finally effected, after that about 600 houses had been burnt or blown up."

What the Great Fire of ten years earlier had done to the other portion of London, so this of Southwark did, on a smaller, but still formidable, scale, to that on the Surrey shore. That incendiarism was suspected, if not proved, is evidenced by the following extract from the diary of the Rev. John Ward: " Grover and his Irish ruffians burnt Southwark and had 1000 pounds for their pains said the narrative of Bedloe. Gifford, a Jesuit, had the management of the fire. The 26th of May 1676 was the dismal fire of Southwark. The fire begunne att one Mr. Welsh, an oilman, near St. Margaret's Hill, betwixt the George and Talbot innes, as Bedloe [1] in his narration relates."

The King's Head, which was, as I have said, one of the old inns destroyed in this holocaust, stood a little further to the east and therefore nearer London Bridge than the two to which I have already referred; but

---

[1] This was Captain William Bedloe, who wrote *A Narrative of the Popish Plot*, 1679; he was also the author of a surprising *Life and Death* of himself, in which, says Lowndes, " the gallanteries and rogueries recorded beggar description." He was hardly, perhaps, a trustworthy authority on the causes of the Southwark fire.

it was only slightly so in the case of the White Hart, on whose inner yard the back portion of it abutted. The inn stood on a site where Roman remains were at one time found in some abundance. Indeed, all this part was occupied by these early invaders, and were excavations able to be carried on in Southwark with the completeness they have been elsewhere, there is little doubt that remarkable results would be shown in this direction.

When exactly the King's Head was established is not recorded, but as it appears to have been an inn of good repute in the closing years of the sixteenth century, it was probably considerably earlier than that period that it came into being. Indeed, there is a circumstance that places its origin before the Reformation; for it is known to have been one of those houses which changed its name at that time, and from the Pope's Head blossomed forth into the King's Head; and an old deed, communicated to Dr. Philip Norman by the late G. Eliot-Hodgkin, whose family owned the property for many years, and dated 1559, informs us that in that year John Gresham and John White, respectively Lord Mayors of London in 1547 and 1563, agreed to pay a sum of money to Thomas Cure for the inn then described as "formerly known as the Popes hed, now as le Kynges hed, abutting on the highway called Longe Southwarke." Later the place became the property of the Humbles, a once well-known Southwark family from whom the Earl of Dudley descends.

Before the fire of 1676 the rent of the inn had been £66 per annum; but after that disaster it was reduced to £38, in consideration of the then tenant, Mary Duffield, rebuilding it in a proper and substantial manner. It continued to flourish, and by the first quarter of the eighteenth century was doing well. Its sign was a half-length portrait of Henry VIII, and Timbs, writing in 1875, says he remembered seeing it, and speaks of it as being well painted.

In 1879, when Crowther made his picture of the King's Head, the actual premises, as well as the yard, were much as they had been in earlier years, although the presence of a new public-house had to some extent interfered with their original picturesqueness. This drawing is one of the most interesting of Crowther's productions, for it not only

MARSHALSEA PLACE
Portion of the Debtors Prison

MARSHALSEA PLACE

Portion of the Debtors Prison

shows the old inn buildings, but also the curious character of the balustrades of the galleries which have an almost celestial air about them, very alien from what one might expect to find in Southwark, but which would be not out of place, say in Chinatown. Whether the influence of Sir William Chambers, after his return from the East and the publication of his *Designs of Chinese Buildings*, extended so far as to affect the architecture of a Southwark inn is a question; but there is no doubt that the drawings he brought back did set a fashion, as may be seen in some of Chippendale's furniture, for instance.

If it were responsible for the galleries of the King's Head we can date these approximately soon after 1757, in which year Chambers's work was published.

Crowther's picture (which, by the way, was exhibited at the Royal Academy in 1887) was executed in 1879. By 1884 a considerable portion of the galleried building had been pulled down, and five years later the whole was demolished. The upper portion was of wood, but the roof was covered with red tiles. There is a remarkable and quite charming variety about the designs of the crossed woodwork forming the balustrades, which were probably unique in London. The one touch of modernity in the picture is the bracket-lamp which gave light to the information that the King's Head was "comfortable," although one is bound to say its appearance, picturesque as it is, rather belies the statement.

The last of the old Southwark inns of which Crowther has left us an illustration is the Queen's Head. It stood on the south of the famous Tabard, and occupied the site of an earlier tavern known variously as the Crowned or the Cross Keys. In the fifteenth century it belonged to the Poynings family, and at one time would appear to have been their private residence, for a letter from Elizabeth Poynings (the daughter of Sir John Paston and widow of Robert Poynings) is dated from there in 1468. In the early years of the sixteenth century the Poynings seem to have given up the house as a place of abode, and to have let it at the rate of £4 a year. After being occupied in various ways—in 1529 it was used as a store for some of the royal armour—it first swims into our ken as a tavern when, in 1558, one Richard Westray, who had apparently been carrying it on as such, bequeathed it to his wife, it then being described as his " messuage called the Cross Kayes, with the brewhouse, garden and stable, as it is now newly builded by his son Thomas."

Without insinuating that the Cross Keys was at this time anything but a regular and well conducted tavern, it is a fact that this particular sign is amongst those which Stow records as being painted on the walls of certain notorious houses in Southwark as an indication of their *raison d'être*.

When exactly the name was changed is uncertain, but Dr. Norman is of opinion that it was about 1635-7, what time one John Harvard or Harvye was its proprietor, this Harvard being none other than the original begetter of Harvard College. The Queen's Head (so now to call it) had come to him through his mother. It was one of the few inns in this neighbourhood that escaped the great fire of 1676, and the reason for this immunity was probably the blowing up of some of the tenements adjoining it, in order to lessen the extent of the disaster.

That by the close of the seventeenth century the tavern was still a well known one and much resorted to may be inferred from the lines in a rare tract published in 1691, and entitled, " The Last Search after Claret in Southwark, or a Visitation of the Vintners of the Mint," which runs as follows:

> To the Queen's-head we hastened, and found the House ring,
> By Broom-men a singing old Simon the King;
> Besides at the bar we perceived a poor Trooper—
> Was cursing his master and calling him Cooper.

Down, indeed, to the middle of the nineteenth century the Queen's Head remained very little altered, except that certain portions of it were then occupied by a hop-merchant. This part was that where the old characteristic galleries ran; and in course of time and following the precedent of other Southwark inns, these were let off in tenements—the open galleries adapting themselves to such uses, and, indeed, being to some extent copied in certain modern model-dwellings. Some thirty years later, *i.e.*, in 1886, changes of a structural kind began to stultify the old-world appearance of the place, and the substitution of a slate roof

ANGEL COURT

With portion of the Marshalsea Prison Wall

ANGEL COURT

With portion of the Marshalsea Prison Wall

for the earlier tiled one was among the alterations. When, too, the plaster with which the walls had been covered was removed it was found that it had overlaid solid oak beams.

Before the coming of the slate roof Crowther luckily made his drawing of the house, which I may parenthetically state was closed in 1895, although the galleried portion remained till a few years later. The premises, in course of time, became a railway depot. This fate overtook others of the old Southwark taverns—a sort of apostolic succession from the old coaching days with which they were at one time so largely identified.

Crowther has left two pictures of the Queen's Head. The first shows it looking east, and it is a curious thing that the artist has not included the cupola of Guy's Hospital, which could be seen above the archway at no great distance off. The similarity of the galleried portion to that at the George will be observed, except that an iron balustrade here has been substituted for the old wooden one on the first floor. Through the archway was that portion of the house which forms the subject of the second picture. We can see the galleried portion in the distance, on the right, and also the modern building which had been erected at the end of the yard. Another modern touch is given to the picture by the structure in the foreground on the left. These utilitarian, ugly erections, however, do but accentuate the old-world charm of what had come down from earlier times, but which circumstance compelled us to disregard and destroy.

It is not uncharacteristic of the curious antitheses one comes across in this part of London that after dealing with taverns we should be brought face to face with a prison. Every reader of Dickens's *Little Dorrit* knows that the Marshalsea, which figures so largely in that book, and the Queen's Bench, with which he was personally so closely concerned, occupied positions in the heart of this area, and cast their baneful influence over the neighbourhood somewhat as the Fleet once did over Ludgate Hill and its immediate vicinity.

Such gaols as these bore out, I think, the remark which Dr. Johnson once enunciated regarding prisons in general as they were in his time: "There," he remarked, "the lewd inflame the lewd, the wicked encourage the wicked; and where a criminal is taught to do that with more cunning which he had been used to do with less."

Although the associations of taverns and prisons may appear incongruous, one of the latter was actually an outcome of an inn, for the White Lion Prison had originally been the White Lion Tavern, and was turned to its later uses about the middle of the sixteenth century. Stow, writing in 1598, thus refers to it: "The 'White Lion' is a gaol," he says, "so called for that the same was a common hostelrie for the receipt of travellers by that sign. This house," he adds, "was first used as a gaol within these forty years last, since the which time the prisoners were once removed thence to an house in Newtowne [Newington], where they remained for a short time, and were returned back again to the aforesaid White Lion, there to remain as in the appointed gaol for the county of Surrey."

The White Lion consequently finds itself in those lines by John Taylor, the water poet, in which he enumerates the five prisons formerly existing in Southwark:

Five jayles or prisons are in Southwarke placed,
The Counter once St. Margaret's church defaced,
The Marshalsea, the King's Bench, and White Lyon,
Then there's the Clinke where handsome lodgings be.

The White Lion in those days appertained to the Priory of St. Mary Overy, and was continued in use as a place of confinement, at least down to 1640, for in that year we are told the apprentices in one of their fits of moral indignation, broke into it and released the whole of the prisoners. It was, no doubt, this incident that made the authorities realize that it was no safe place for the incarceration of evil doers, with the result that from being a regular prison it was, towards the close of the seventeenth century, converted into a House of Correction.

The interior depicted by Crowther represents one of the portions of the White Lion that still existed in 1887, and which had apparently been incorporated with the Marshalsea of *Little Dorrit*. Thence it may have been that the Dorrit family passed out into the liberty and temporary prosperity of the great world. This wooden walled room represented in

86

QUEEN'S BENCH PRISON—THE CANTEEN

1879

THE CANTEEN IN THE QUEEN'S BENCH PRISON

any case a phase of the social life of the period which is happily with yesterday's seven thousand years: when what was often due to misfortune was punished as if it were a crime; when a debtor was prevented from doing anything towards paying his creditors, and was herded indifferently with others who were actually criminals or were as unfortunate as himself.

It was on part of the site of the old White Lion Prison that the later Marshalsea (not to be confounded with the earlier gaol of the same name) was erected in 1811. It was this Marshalsea that has been made familiar to us by Dickens, who was himself, as a boy, lodging in Lant Street, familiar with it. Anything that Dickens has written about the London with which he was personally acquainted is welcome in these days when so relatively few of such relics survive, and I, therefore, make no apology for giving here his description of the place as he remembered it when writing in the year 1856.

" Thirty years ago," he says, " there stood, a few doors short of the church of St. George, in the borough of Southwark, on the left-hand side of the way going southward, the Marshalsea Prison. It had stood there many years before, and it remained there some years afterwards; but it is gone now, and the world is none the worse without it. It was an oblong pile of barrack building, partitioned into squalid houses standing back to back, so that there were no back rooms; environed by a narrow paved yard hemmed in by high walls duly spiked at top. Itself a close and confined prison for debtors, it contained within it a much closer and more confined gaol for smugglers. Offenders against the revenue laws, and defaulters to excise or customs, who had incurred fines which they were unable to pay, were supposed to be incarcerated behind an iron-plated door, closing up a second prison consisting of a strong cell or two and a blind alley some yard and a half wide which formed the mysterious termination of the very limited skittle-ground in which the Marshalsea debtors bowled down their troubles. Supposed to be incarcerated there because the time had rather outgrown the strong cells and the blind alley. In practice they had come to be considered a little too bad, though in theory they were quite as good as ever. . . . Hence the smugglers habitually consorted with the debtors (who received them with open arms), except at certain constitutional moments when somebody came from some office, to go through some form of overlooking something, which neither he nor anybody else knew anything about."

When Dickens was examining the neighbourhood, in order to refresh his mind with the details of the place which he had once known so well, he was able, as he himself tells us in the preface to *Little Dorrit*, to discover little except certain lower portions of the old walls, the narrow yard, and a few of the original paving-stones which were then defying time and the housebreaker " in Marshalsea Place, turning out of Angel Court leading to Bermondsey."

Crowther's pictures of the Marshalsea Prison as it appeared in 1887 are interesting reminders of what the interior and exterior of the place must have looked like when Dickens visited it some thirty years earlier. The picture representing the " sky-parlour " might well be the room in which, in Phiz's well-known illustration, Little Dorrit is gazing in a day-dream out of the diminutive dormer window; the other shows another side of the prison in Marshalsea Place.

To-day there is nothing to recall the structure except the name of Marshalsea Road, linking up the Borough High Street with the Southwark Bridge Road, on the opposite side of the way, and a little further south from where the Marshalsea of Dickens, *alias* the earlier White Lion Prison, once stood.

It is important to distinguish clearly between the positions of the two Marshalsea prisons, because much confusion has arisen in the descriptions given of them (notably in *London Past and Present*) by the supposition that each of them occupied the same site. The fact is that the earlier of them (which eventually developed into the King's Bench and later the Queen's Bench) stood on the right-hand side of the Borough High Street (going south) at the point where it branches off in one direction into the Borough Road, and in the other into Newington Causeway; the spot, in a word, where the King's Bench is shown on Horwood's plan of London.

The later Marshalsea was, as we have seen Dickens stating, " a few doors short of the church of St. George," just beyond Layton's Yard and Angel Court, which Crowther shows us as it was in 1887, in the accompanying picture. It ran along the north side of the Marshalsea Prison, the

QUEEN'S BENCH PRISON—THE CHAPEL

THE CHAPEL IN THE QUEEN'S BENCH PRISON

QUEEN'S BENCH PRISON—THE PRISONERS' YARD

wall of which (shown on the right) overlooked it. It led from the Borough High Street, between what were then Nos. 146 and 147 in that thoroughfare, into an alley abutting on some tenements known as Colliers' Rents.

When the earlier Marshalsea was actually established in Southwark is not recorded, but it is known to have been in existence in the time of Edward III and to have been destroyed by the Kentish rebels in 1381. By the time of Queen Elizabeth the Marshalsea had become the second in importance of the five State prisons, that in the Tower alone being greater. One of the reasons for this, besides the size of the place, was no doubt the fact that "the Court of the Marshalsea" was connected with it, a court which, presided over by the steward and marshal of the King's house, as those officials were termed, held jurisdiction over all offences committed within the verge or, in other words, within a radius of twelve miles round the royal residence. As in the time of James I disputes as to this widespread power arose, the King, on Bacon's advice, created, in 1611, another centre for the settling of such differences, known as the Court of Verge whose powers were, however, much more restricted, as they were confined to an area surrounding Whitehall, as far as St. James's, although the Parks were included. A gaol enquiry, held in 1729, laid it down that "the prison of the Marshalsea doth belong to the Court of Marshalsea of the King's Household and to the Court of Record of the King's Palace of Westminster"; and it, therefore, had a very special and official position very different from that of a mere prison such as its successor alone was. But these powers were, in 1801, removed from Southwark to Scotland Yard, and were finally abolished about half a century later.

The King's (or, later, Queen's) Bench Prison originally stood just to the south of the later (or Dickens's) Marshalsea. In Rocque's plan of 1746 it is shown with its long buildings on each side of which ran King's Bench Alley and Bridewell Alley respectively, abutting on the main thoroughfare. Behind it was a large irregular piece of ground planted with trees and overlooking open fields and, beyond, the Tenter Ground. About ten years after this, however, as I have stated, the prison was removed to a spot at the junction of what is now Borough High Street with the Borough Road and Newington Causeway. In 1780 the Gordon

89

Rioters burnt it; but it was subsequently rebuilt and was then surrounded by a very high wall which effectually prevented its inmates from seeing anything of the open country and green fields which were then close by, although anyone walking in this neighbourhood to-day will have difficulty in realizing it. When the Act for abolishing arrest for debt became law the prison was closed, although it was subsequently used as a place of incarceration for military offenders.

The list of those who have been detained here is a long one, and contains illustrious names ranging from those of Henry, Prince of Wales (afterwards Henry V), through such later ones as Rushworth and Baxter, Theodore, King of Corsica, and Smollett, Lord Cochrane, and William Combe (of Dr. Syntax fame), Benjamin Robert Haydon (who painted his " Mock Election " here), and William Hone, who here completed the compilation of his *Every Day Book*. Besides such as these Mr. Micawber was once shut up here and was duly visited by little David, what time Mrs. Micawber was in lodgings in adjacent Lant Street; while Madelaine Bray's father, it will be remembered by readers of *Nicholas Nickleby*, lived in one of a row of mean and not over-cleanly houses situated within " the rules " of the prison. Tallis, in his *London Street Views*, shows the spike-surmounted wall which then (1838-9) surrounded the building, and in his accompanying notes remarks that those who are able " to purchase the liberties have the benefit of walking through Blackman Street, a part of the Borough, and in St. George's Fields." Dickens elsewhere likens the King's Bench to the home of dry rot among men under an old bad system of legislation.

The three illustrations of the King's Bench Prison which, since 1837, had of course become the Queen's Bench, which Crowther produced in 1879, the year in which the building was demolished, afford us an excellent idea of the various features of that place. The first represents the Canteen, an ancient building which had obviously been adapted to such purposes, and whose relatively modern doorway and window were strangely out of place in their otherwise monkish environment. No doubt, too, the flooring had been raised, as the bases of the pillars do not appear.

Another picture shows the little chapel which stood at the north-west angle of the prison, abutting on Belvidere Place, now absorbed in the Southwark Bridge Road. Crowther made his drawing of this feature of

OLD HOUSES IN SNOWFIELDS, BERMONDSEY

the Queen's Bench in 1879, the year in which it was demolished. This chapel appears rather obviously to have been formed out of a room (perhaps a court-room) originally conftructed for other purposes. It has a late Georgian air about it, in curious contradiftinction to the mediaevalism of the Canteen.

The laft picture is that of the interior of the prison yard, with the main buildings ftretching from the right-hand side across the background, and the high wall, with the spikes removed, showing on the left. The entrance is seen in the diftance, and in the foreground is the pump. It was to one of those rooms that David Copperfield went to borrow a knife and fork from Captain Hopkins; and in another, that of Captain Porter, that the famous " petition " was ftretched out for signature on an ironing board, and read with much unction by the gallant officer on anyone showing the slighteft disposition to hear it, what time its compiler, Mr. Micawber or Mr. Dickens, senior, which you will, liftened " with a little of an author's vanity, and contemplated (not severely) the spikes on the opposite wall."

Rather to the north of Angel Court, of which I have already spoken, runs Newcomen Street, or King Street, as it was formerly called; this leads into Snowfields, which links it up with Bermondsey Street. This Snowfields is now a thickly populated area and as innocent of fields as it is of mountains. In earlier days, in fact when Horwood produced his plan at the end of the eighteenth century, it was known as Snow's Fields —and was even then lined with houses on both sides; although on the south of it, beyond the buildings, was a good deal of open ground cut up into rope-walks and tanning yards and so forth.

Once all this part was low-lying ground, a marsh when the tide was out, a lake when it was in; but draining and embanking have long since overcome the influence of the river, and Bermondsey may ftill be regarded as the headquarters of tanners and rope-makers who carry on their trade in a more sophifticated environment than that which their predecessors knew. Thus it is that the Snowfields of to-day connotes a long ftreet of dwellings, whereas the Snow's Fields of the earlier eighteenth century was largely rural, although not by any means entirely innocent of bricks and mortar.

Anyone who likes can penetrate the congeries of mean ftreets which form what is generically known as Bermondsey, stretching east and south of the Borough High Street, from which Tooley Street debouches close to the river, and Bermondsey Street descends thence to Long Lane. Once, in the January of 1665-6, Mr. Secretary Pepys, accompanied by Lord Brouncker, found himself in this then water-logged locality; and his picture of it forms a curious antithesis to what obtains there to-day. " Lord! " he exclaims, " what a dirty walk we had, and so strong the wind, that in the fields we many times could not carry our bodies against it, but were driven backwards. We went through Horsly Downe, where I never was since a boy. . . . It was dangerous to walk the streets, the bricks and tiles falling from the houses, that the whole streets were covered with them; and whole chimneys, nay, whole houses, in two or three places, blowed down. . . ."

Had Pepys turned down Bermondsey Street, from the Tooley Street by which he and his companion made their way to London Bridge, he would have come, before he had proceeded far, to Bermondsey Abbey, which stood roughly where Abbey Street is now, its precincts spreading a considerable way northward. Wilkinson, in his *Londina Illustrata*, gives a full-page picture representing Bermondsey Abbey as it appeared in 1805. The artist, Whicelo, was obviously largely drawing on his imagination, and was representing the Abbey as it might have been in 1605, but could certainly not have looked like two hundred years later. For here we see it surrounded by open country, whereas in Horwood's plan of a slightly earlier date this area is shown as being then largely built over, although not, of course, to anything like the extent it is in the present day.

In his letterpress Wilkinson states that " in the year 1810 there were a great many fragments of the venerable foundation of Bermondsey Abbey remaining, probably more than almost any religious edifice in or near London, owing to its remote situation, which has caused fewer improvements in the building line (that worst enemy to our architectural antiquities) than elsewhere "; and he mentions specifically the Gate House as being then nearly entire, as indeed it is shown in Whicelo's reconstruction; together with various other structural remains. What I think probable is that the artist has reproduced what actually still stood

92

ANCIENT TENEMENTS IN BERMONDSEY STREET

in his day, although in a ruinous condition (which he has cleverly camouflaged), and has, in place of the then existing and more modern buildings that surround it, drawn the open fields with their rustic lanes and their trees as they no doubt were at a much earlier date.

But after all this is to consider Bermondsey Street and its purlieus as they appeared in very remote times. Crowther's picture of the thoroughfare, which was executed in 1886, shows it as it was just forty years ago; and those who are acquainted with this area as it exists, will not need to be told what changes have taken place here.

The charming little picture which the artist made of Snowfields, shows it at the point where certain timbered houses then stood, with their high tiled roofs and little dormer windows. The block was a very attractive one, and indeed was only spoilt by the later rebuilding of the house in the middle distance at the corner of the thoroughfare known as Crosby Road. Even this, however, looks old and quaint by the side of the newly built gin-palace in the foreground on the right, and the obviously modern shops (happily we can see nothing of them but their fore-shortened fronts) on the left. The picture was executed in 1887, and how modernized has become this quarter may be realized when one finds a thoroughfare a little further along Snowfields called Kipling Street.

Another view of this quarter is shown us in the next picture, which represents Bermondsey Street as it was in 1886. It would be hard to find to-day anything in London quite like this collocation of ancient houses, which existed here these forty years ago. They seem to be gradually pressing the long-suffering little shops beneath into the earth, and themselves to be but kept together by the plaster which over-laid the half-timbered fronts of a former day. The upper portions had evidently been turned to use, probably as a tannery, as we can see by the air slits introduced beneath the gables. They were relics of the time when Bermondsey Abbey dominated this quarter. One thinks that the passage of a single motorbus, were they standing now, would bring the whole block clattering to the ground. Crowther, perhaps with his tongue in his cheek, has extended his picture in order to include a modern tavern at the right hand—to show no doubt how greatly the nineteenth century had advanced architecturally.

CHAPTER VI

STOCKWELL, VAUXHALL, AND BATTERSEA

ON our way back to the westerly portion of the Surrey side of the river, where pictures of Lambeth await us, we have to retrace our steps through the Borough proper, from which we have wandered somewhat in visiting Snowfields. We can do this by going along Union Street and Charlotte Street into the Blackfriars Road, which used, by the way, to be called Great Surrey Street. At this point we have the Surrey Chapel at the corner of the thoroughfare on our right, of which Crowther made the accompanying picture in 1881. The history of this building is so interesting that we may well stop a little to talk about it.

It forms a curious antithesis to the old red-brick, timbered, begalleried inns which we have been considering, and its appearance denotes at once that classic convention which had, and still has, such a vogue in London. The chapel was closed for religious uses in 1881. As it had been begun in 1782, in which year Rowland Hill laid its first stone, it had nearly reached a century of religious activity; and had for many years been the scene of fervid eloquence on the part of the founder and his coadjutors, and often of the former's abundant wit and sarcasm.

It still stands, although in a vastly changed neighbourhood and turned to alien uses, but beneath it (where the pulpit formerly stood) the body of Rowland Hill was buried! He himself once lived next door, probably in the house shown in the background of Crowther's picture. Besides ministering to the spiritual wants of his large congregations in his own whimsical way, he studied their bodily needs, and having become acquainted with Jenner, he was so struck by that great man's discovery that he practised vaccination in the chapel itself, and is said to have personally inoculated over ten thousand persons there.

The chapel was, from its shape, known as the Rotunda Chapel, and

THE SURREY CHAPEL, BLACKFRIARS ROAD

as such is mentioned in Thackeray's *Sketches and Travels in London*, where Mr. Brown, senior, become reminiscent, it will be recalled, tells how he used to accompany an aunt thither, in the year 1811, "when the Comet was." There is an extant print of the place as it appeared three years after this, and we see stately carriages putting down members of the congregation at its door. Among these were such as the Duke of Kent, William Wilberforce, Dean Milner, and much fashionable company drawn thither by the fame of the preacher. One of the carriages may be Rowland Hill's own, for he is known to have used one (before, apparently, he lived next door) and about this a tale is told.

Some one who thought it inappropriate for a clergyman thus to arrive at his chapel sent him a notice to be read out to the effect that " The prayers of the congregation are desired for the Rev. Rowland Hill, that he will not go riding in his carriage on Sundays." Nothing daunted, Hill read aloud the message, and then, looking up, gravely added: " If the writer of this piece of folly and impertinence is in the congregation and will go into the vestry after service, and let me put a saddle on his back, I will ride him home instead of going in my carriage "; and he proceeded with the service as if nothing had happened. He afterwards remarked to someone who reminded him of the circumstance: " You know I could not call him an ass in plain terms."

But if one begins recalling anecdotes of Rowland Hill and his innumerable memorabilia one would never have done. After a long life (he died in 1833 in his eighty-ninth year) in doing good all over the country as well as in his chapel, he has left the reputation of an outspoken exceedingly humorous, upright, and earnest worker in the vast field of religious and social reform; and may be in this respect bracketed with such outstanding men as Wesley and Whitfield.

When he was about erecting his chapel he received support and contributions from many who were not of his particular persuasion (he was actually of the Established Church, but was described as a Calvanistic Methodist), among them being Lord George Gordon and Lady Huntingdon; and the chapel, which cost some £5,000, was opened in the June of 1783.

In 1823 Southey paid a visit here, and in a letter describes his experiences; and as he incidentally gives a picture of the interior as well as of Hill himself, I transcribe his words:

" Rowland Hill's pulpit is raised very high," he writes, " and before it, at about half the height, is the reader's desk on his right and the clerk's on his left—the clerk being a very grand personage, with a sonorous voice. The singing was so general and so good that I joined in it. During the singing, after Rowland had made his prayer before the sermon, we were beckoned from our humble places by a gentleman in one of the pews. He was very civil. Rowland, a fine, tall old man, with strong features, very like his portrait, began by reading three verses from his text, stooping to the book in a very peculiar manner. Having done this, he stood up erect and said, ' Why, the text *is* a sermon, and a very weighty one too.' I could not always follow his delivery, the loss of his teeth rendering his words sometimes indistinct, and the more so because his pronunciation is peculiar, generally giving *e* the sound of *ai*, like the French. His manner was striking and animated, sometimes impressive and dignified, always remarkable, and so powerful a voice I have rarely or ever heard. Sometimes he took off his spectacles, frequently stooped down to read a text, and on these occasions he seemed to double his body, so high did he stand. He told one or two familiar stories and used some odd expressions, such as, ' A murrain on those who preach that when we are sanctified we do not grow in grace! ' And again, ' I had almost said I had rather see the devil in the pulpit than an Antinomian.' The purport of his sermon was good; nothing fanatical, nothing enthusiastic, and the Calvanism it expressed was so qualified as to be harmless. The manner that of a performer, as great in his line as Kean or Kemble: and the manner it is which has attracted so large a congregation about him all of the better order of persons in business."

The humorous, persuasive eloquence of its protagonist—the fearless, outspoken character of his comments on men and matters, and something dynamic in the man himself, made the Surrey Chapel a magnet which drew to it all sorts and conditions of people. Nothing quite like it had been seen in London since Whitfield electrified his hearers by his eloquence or Wesley by his simple powers of persuasion drew them to him; nothing was to equal Rowland Hill's powers of what may be termed religious cajolery until Spurgeon, with something of the same attributes, hypnotized his generation by not dissimilar methods.

The Surrey Chapel had for long become, to use the words of Edward Walford, " the centre of a system of benevolent societies designed to reach the various classes of the community, and after Rowland Hill's death in 1833 the work was carried on by the Rev. James Sherman till 1854, when the Rev. Newman Hall resuscitated something of the old atmosphere by his energetic and eloquent preaching."

If the Surrey Chapel has become secularized, another chapel (which somehow one always associates with it, although it was far enough away in Clerkenwell) developed out of anything but an ecclesiastical origin. For the Spa Fields Chapel had once been a Pantheon, a humble imitator of the famous one in Oxford Street. It was a rather notorious place, and when in 1774 its proprietor became bankrupt, it was sold to a group of people who opened it as a Church of England chapel in 1777. Subsequently the Countess of Huntingdon bought it and turned it into a Dissenting chapel. An old print of it, dated 1781, shows its rotunda, with a smaller castellated circular building on one side and a curious semicircular entrance in front. Lady Huntingdon, by the way, lived in a house adjoining. It so happens that among the topographical pictures left by Crowther is one of this chapel as it was in 1886; and although this is in a different quarter of the city from that with which we are here concerned, this interesting illustration is given as a pendant to that of the Surrey chapel.

By this drawing we see how the original building had been enlarged and improved by the addition of a classic portico of solid construction. Behind it, on the right, appears the castellated portion of the edifice to which I have referred; but the old entrance has been wholly absorbed in the new work. A comparison of Crowther's picture with the 1781 print, will reveal various other alterations; but the residence of Lady Huntingdon, which was close to the chapel on the left, is only indicated by a chimney-stack and a small portion of one of the walls.

Crowther found the subjects for his next two pictures (*vide Plates*) in Lambeth. That area is little known to the Londoner, and probably, with the exception of the red-brick archiepiscopal palace and its neighbouring church, there are few parts of the metropolis of which the past history is so nebulous in the minds of the general citizen, as is that of this area which cannot be said exactly to be outlying, but which, in consequence of the systematic disregard we have shown for the south bank of the Thames, is certainly more or less of a *terra incognita*. That being so, something beyond merely a general illustrative note to Crowther's pictures seems to be called for; and I shall, therefore, attempt a fuller description of the area than has been necessary in the case of more familiar ones.

Etymologists have been at some pains to explain the meaning of the word Lambeth. In Wagner's *Names and their Meanings*, which follows Taylor's *Words and Places*, it is given with some assurance as being a corruption of Loamhithe, the Anglo-Saxon for haven of the loamy soil; but Lysons, while remarking that " the name has been variously written in public records and by the ancient historians," notes that in the earliest extant document in which it is mentioned, it is written Lambehith; and he proceeds to say that " in Doomsday Book it is given probably by a clerical error as Lanchei," and that " in the ancient historians it is spelt Lamhee, Lamheth, Lambyth, Lamedh, and with many other variations, some of which were probably occasioned by the errors of transcribers." Most etymologists derive the name, he says, from Lam, dirt, and Hyd or Hythe, a haven; and this I am inclined to think the most probable solution when one remembers that in those days all the foreshore and much of the land beyond was then subject to the overflowing of an unrestrained river, and must have presented much the same dirty appearance as does the foreshore to-day when the tide is low.

Lambeth is divided into two distinct areas, north and south; the former running by the river and including the Palace and so forth; the latter embracing Vauxhall and Stockwell. The northern portion passed as a gift from the Countess Goda, a sister of Edward the Confessor, to the see of Rochester which, in the year 1197, exchanged it with the see of Canterbury, for the Manor of Dartford (then written Darente). The south portion was in those early days held by the monks of Waltham from Harold and Edward the Confessor.

Although the see of Rochester gave up its rights here to that of

SPA FIELDS CHAPEL

SPA FIELDS CHAPEL

Canterbury, it reserved a piece of ground near the church on which a residence was built known as La Place, and subsequently, when it was given to the Bishop of Carlisle by Henry VIII in exchange for that prelate's former residence in the Strand, it was known as Carlisle House —a structure that remained in existence, more or less in its old form, till 1827, when it was demolished.

It was here, by the way, in 1531, during the residence of Bishop Fisher, that an attempt was made by a man named Rose to poison him. The bishop escaped, but two servants died from the effects of eating the poisoned dish, and Rose was " boiled alive " at Smithfield.

There was, too, in the grounds of Carlisle House an extraordinarily fine mulberry tree about which Oldys, the antiquary, waxed enthusiastic, and which went by the name of Queen Elizabeth's mulberry.

When all this part was subsequently developed, Carlisle Street and Hercules Buildings perpetuated the site of the former mansion, and ran through its gardens, just as Norfolk Row marked the spot where the Howards had a residence hereabouts in the sixteenth century.

Although Lambeth Palace resumes in itself the most interesting associations ecclesiastical or otherwise of this part of London, there have in the past been many notable people associated with Lambeth's long secular history. And we are able to go back even to pre-Conquest days to find that Hardicanute died here in 1042, during the celebration of the marriage feast of the son of one of his nobles, at which he was present. Whether poison or intemperance was the cause is a moot point, but the King had just risen to drink the bride's health when he fell back in a fit and expired after fearful agony.

It is said, too, that it was at Lambeth that Harold, the son of Earl Godwin, placed the crown which he had usurped after the death of Edward the Confessor, on his head; while we hear of Henry III celebrating the Christmas of 1231 here; and the next year of a Parliament being held here. As there was a palace at Kennington it is likely, as Lysons surmises, that that building was the scene of these events.

The history of Lambeth Palace, as well as that of the church, do not come within my scope, and as both have been exhaustively dealt with there is no need even to summarize their annals. But it will be interesting to notice some of the former notable inhabitants of this district, especially as two of them, Sir Noel de Caron and John Tradescant, are intimately associated with buildings of which Crowther has left us pictures, here reproduced.

For some reason or other Lambeth seems to have been a favourite dwelling place for those astrologers who, in the fifteenth and sixteenth centuries, made so good a living from the credulity of the people as well as that of their rulers. Dr. Dee lived at Mortlake; but another notable exponent of the art, Simon Forman, is said, on the authority of a yet better known one, William Lilly, to have resided in Lambeth and, indeed, to have died suddenly in a boat on the river close by, on 2nd September 1611, at the exact hour and on the day he had himself predicted on the Sunday before that event. Lysons gives the story in his account of Forman's life and death, a story he took from Lilly's *Life and Times*, wherein it first appeared.

A contemporary of Forman's in Lambeth was one Captain Bubb, who lived in Lambeth Marsh. He was not so successful a practitioner as the better known man however; indeed, he was not unacquainted with the pillory, and " ended his days in disgrace " according to Lilly. Yet another Lambeth astrologer was one whose name is better remembered than either of these, for he was no less a personage than Francis Moore— the " Old Moore " of the original almanack, which still survives. The church registers reveal, too, the presence here of many people who, if not exactly notable, were locally known to fame; and in addition there appear some names which are recognized more widely, such as those of Robert Barker, of panorama fame, who died here in 1806; Peter Dollond, the optician, whose decease at the age of ninety took place in 1820; Sowerby, the writer on natural history, and Patrick Nasmyth, the landscape painter—" the English Hobbema," as he has been called; John Broughton, the prize-fighter, and Parsons, the actor.

What the writer in *London Past and Present* says about the Lambeth of 1891 may be predicated of the place in 1926: " The district attached to the mother church, Lambeth Proper, is a manufacturing and densely populated place. There are breweries, distilleries, engineers' yards gasworks, and other large establishments, but the most distinctive,

HOUSES ON WEST SIDE OF CHURCH STREET, LAMBETH

perhaps, are the potteries, in which are wrought every description of earthenware from drain pipes to the most refined articles of ornamental art. The establishment of Messrs. Doulton, near the palace, will well repay a visit. The building is noteworthy for the elaborate designs in terra-cotta which adorn the exterior, whilst the showrooms contain choice specimens of the hand-wrought and hand-painted ' Lambeth Faience,' and ' Doulton Ware,' which promise to maintain a special place in the art of the modern potter."

Besides such utilitarian and artistic features all this part has in the past been closely associated with amusement in its varied forms, and from Cuper's Gardens and Astley's and Vauxhall to Kennington Oval, there has been along this south bank an apostolic succession of such things since the early days of the bull- and bear-baiting and the Bankside theatres, which the present desolate, dilapidated state of the foreshore makes it difficult for us to realize.

One of Crowther's pictures of this district represents the old houses on the west side of Church Street, Lambeth, as they appeared about the year 1880 (although this sketch is actually undated).

Such a picturesque building as is here shown almost asked for demolition at a time when some of the most charming bits of old London were ruthlessly destroyed; and its approaching fate is foreseen on the left-hand side where a probably not dissimilar structure had been pulled down. By the large opening in its centre it would seem to have once been a tavern, and this the entrance to its yard. Later, no doubt, dwellings had been erected on this site and the entrance had been converted into a passage-way leading to them, as is indicated by the two posts. The shop fronts were distinguishing features when Crowther made his drawing; while the red-tiled roof, with its three dormer windows, was another even more noticeable one. At the right hand of the picture, in the distance, can be seen the spire of St. Mark's Church, Kennington.

Among the past residents of Lambeth few were better known in their own day or have left more tangible evidence of their busy existence, than that John Tradescant whose museum was the wonder and delight of an earlier generation. Visitors to Oxford are familiar with the collections which, having been given to Elias Ashmole, are now to be seen together with the portraits of the Tradescant family, in the Ashmolean Museum.

The mansion occupied by Tradescant was known as Turret House, and what it looked like not long before its demolition, can be judged by Crowther's picture. It stood to the south of Beaufoy's Distillery (which had been moved hither from Cuper's Gardens) which it adjoined, and as the Distillery was on the site of Caron or Carron House these two notable Lambeth mansions were in close proximity to each other. The house, according to Walford, was a plain brick building, with a courtyard in front and large iron gates, and there was attached to it the physic-garden which the Tradescants had established in England at a period when few such places were to be met with in this country.

Izaak Walton, in his *Compleat Angler*, has the following interesting reference to Tradescant's collections: " I know," he writes, " we islanders are averse to the belief of wonders; but there be so many strange creatures now to be seen, many collected by John Tradescant, and others added by my friend Elias Ashmole, Esq., who now keeps them carefully and methodically at his house near to Lambeth, near London, as may yet get belief of some of the other wonders I mentioned. I will tell you some of the wonders you may now see, and not till then believe, unless you think fit. You may see there the hog-fish, the dog-fish, the dolphin, the coney-fish, the parrot-fish, the shark, the poison-fish, the sword-fish; and not only other incredible fish, but you may see there the salamander, several sorts of barnacles, of Solan geese, and the bird of paradise; such sorts of snakes, and such birds' nests, and of so various forms and so wonderfully made, as may beget wonder and amazement in any beholder; and so many hundreds of other rarities in that collection, as will make the other wonders I spake of the less incredible."

We should, nowadays, hardly be wrought to such enthusiasm as the good Izaak here displays, at the exhibition of what would appear to us very small beer. But we have advanced in knowledge since those simpler days; and not only was Walton an astonished visitor, but royal and illustrious ones came to see the wonders which Tradescant had assembled in his house at Lambeth. Charles I and his queen, Laud and Bucking-ham, and Robert Earl of Salisbury were among such interested visitors;

TURRET HOUSE, SOUTH LAMBETH

P

while John Evelyn, who came to Lambeth to visit his relation, Sir Robert Needham, sometimes dined with Tradescant, and afterwards wandered about his very catholic museum.

The fact is the Tradescants were pioneers as collectors of objects of natural history, and as such may be regarded as the forerunners of men like Ashmole, Hans Sloane, and Ashton Lever.

The garden of Turret House stretched from what is now the Westminster Bridge Road to the South Lambeth Road and was bounded by Mead Place and King Edward Street, formerly George's Row, the whole property of a more or less triangular form lying to the north-west of Bethlehem Hospital. Crowther's picture of the house itself shows what that building looked like in 1880, as well as the rural nature of its surroundings. Only forty-six years have elapsed since this drawing was executed, and it is amazing to think how unspoilt was this area so relatively short a time ago

Although a more particular description of Turret House is now impossible, something should at least be said about the two men (father and son) who were successive occupiers of the mansion, and who here assembled together so notable a collection of curiosities and rarities.

The elder John Tradescant, or Tradeskin, as the name is often found spelt in contemporary records, had been a gardener in the service of the first Duke of Buckingham, whence he passed into that of Charles I. In his search for rare plants on behalf of his royal and noble patrons he travelled extensively not only in Europe, but in Africa, then an arduous and often dangerous undertaking. In this way he gradually accumulated the many strange objects with which his house and garden overflowed. He died in 1638, his wife having predeceased him by four years. His son, another John, carried on his father's work and added to his accumulations; but whether or not he was as ready to exhibit these to all and sundry as his father had been is a question. Certainly Flatman, in one of his poems, remarks:

> Thus John Tradeskin starves our wondering eyes
> By boxing up his new-found rarities,

which would seem to indicate that he was not; while it would appear

103

that he took less care of the paternal trees and shrubs than he did of the museum, for we are told that when, in 1649, Sir William Watson and other members of the Royal Society visited the grounds, they found very few of the trees that had been planted by the elder Tradescant.

However, the younger man was careful enough over the indoor collections, and in 1656 published a little volume entitled *Museum Tradescantium*, with portraits by Hollar of his father and himself, in which his possessions are described. Before he died he and his wife signed a deed of gift of these to their friend Ashmole; so that Dr. Ducarel (who, by the way, lived subsequently in a portion of what had been the Tradescants' house) is wrong in stating that the collection was sold to Ashmole, and not given. It appears, however, that on Tradescant's death in 1642 Ashmole had difficulty with his widow about getting possession of the property, and was obliged to invoke the law before he could live in the house. However, the third John Tradescant having died in 1652, and his mother (the widow referred to) in 1678, Ashmole was able to enter into peaceable occupation; in fact, he appears to have succeeded in doing so four years before the last event occurred. In Lambeth Church may be seen the granite tomb of the Tradescants, with a long inscription which, as it is curious, and resumes in itself the outlines of the family history, may not be regarded as out of place here. After relating the dates of the decease of the members of the family, it proceeds with this rhyming inscription:

> Know, stranger, ere thou pass, beneath this stone
> Lye John Tradescant, Grandsire, Father, and son.
> The last died in his spring; the other two
> Lived till they had travell'd Art and Nature through,
> As by their choice collections may appear,
> Of what is rare in land, in sea, in air;
> Whilst they (as Homer's Iliad in a nut)
> A world of wonders in one closet shut.
> These famous antiquarians that had been
> Both gardeners to the rose and lily queen,
> Transplanted now themselves, sleep here; and when
> Angels shall with their trumpets waken men,
> And fire shall purge the world, these hence shall rise,
> And change this garden for a Paradise.

The elaborate tomb, on which this jingle appears, was originally set up in 1662 by the widow of the younger Tradescant; but being in a state of decay was repaired in 1773; and again entirely restored, under the ægis of Sir William Hooker and others, in 1853.

The other mansion in this neighbourhood of which Crowther has left a picture is that known as Carron, or more properly Caron, House. Its importance is evidenced by the fact that in Ogilby's *Britannia Depicta* it is marked in the plan showing the road out of London leading to Kingston, and is there called Caroone House, the words "Dr. Cheney's School" being inscribed underneath. The builder of this house was a man of importance in his day. He was, indeed, the Sir Noel Caron who, for some thirty-three or four years had been Ambassador from the United Provinces to this country, "in which time," we are told, "he performed that place with much honour and good to his own country and state here." So successfully did he ingratiate himself with the royal family that on the manor of Kennington reverting to the Crown, it was bestowed by Charles, Prince of Wales, afterwards Charles I, on him and Sir Francis Cottington jointly; and in 1618 the former proceeded to erect a fine house here, with two wings, on the front of which appeared the inscription: "Omne solum forti patria."

During Caron's residence here he showed himself generous in his benefactions to the poor, and besides gifts of money, duly recorded in the local annals, he erected in 1622 and endowed, some almshouses for seven poor women, which were "situated near the road leading to Kingston, not far from Vauxhall turnpike," as Lysons tells us. Over the gateway was a Latin inscription indicating that they were founded by Caron in the thirty-second year of his Embassy to England. This benefactor to Lambeth died at his house here on 1st December 1624, and was buried in the chancel of the church, on the following 25th January, his funeral sermon being preached by Archbishop Abbot.

In 1635-6 Caron House was fitted up for the reception of the Ambassador from the King of Poland; but it was destined later to have a more notable occupant, for by letters patent dated 23rd April 1666 Charles II granted it "with the gardens and orchards thereunto belonging" to Lord Chancellor Clarendon. Clarendon did not long occupy the place, however, for in the following year he made it over to Sir Jeremy Whichcott on consideration of the sum of £2,000.

During the Great Fire the prisoners removed from the Fleet were placed in Caron House. By this time the mansion had become rather dilapidated, and much of it appears gradually to have been pulled down and its once ample grounds sadly encroached upon. It is said, indeed, that " all that remained of the house within the present century was taken down in 1809," Lister's *Life of Clarendon* being quoted as the authority for this statement. I am inclined to think, however, that this is hardly correct, as only three years previously (1806) it is known to have been in use as a school—the Dr. Cheney's, in fact, mentioned by Ogilby, as we have seen; and as is obvious from Crowther's picture, what remained of it when he made his sketch in 1887 is of far earlier date than the nineteenth century, although the addition of a modern portico and steps give it a later air. What I think is probable is that what we see here was a small portion of the original ample mansion which had been permitted to remain when the rest of the building was demolished, and which had been brought up to more modern requirements by certain additions and reconstructions. Indeed, it looks like so many early Georgian houses whose original simplicity of outline has been thus interfered with; but I cannot believe that it was wholly designed at a period after the year 1809, in which we are told the whole of Caron House was destroyed.

The original mansion had a centre and two wings in the form of half a Roman H. It would be interesting if its builder could be identified with John Thorpe, who was fond of this design for his structures, and to whom we owe Holland House *inter alia*. The large deer-park attached to Caron House extended as far as Vauxhall and Kennington, and Allen, writing his *History of Surrey* in 1829, states that part of the walls surrounding it was then in existence, " particularly one part across Kennington Oval." This, indeed, brings me to the fact that the Oval absorbed a portion of Sir Noel Caron's pleasance, and where they play cricket to-day he must have walked in the reign of James I, as the great Clarendon did in that of Charles II.

Anyone scouring the thickly populated area now known as Kennington, Vauxhall, and Stockwell, with its closely packed houses will have

CARRON OR CARON HOUSE, VAUXHALL

CARROUN OR CARON HOUSE, VAUXHALL

difficulty in envisaging it as it was down to the opening of the nineteenth century, with its fields and large open spaces and its important mansions standing in their own ample grounds. That considerable building activity had already then taken place is, of course, proved by old plans; but the lesser houses that had been erected bordered on the main thoroughfares running through this large district (many of which still stand exhibiting features which seem curiously alien to their present neighbourhood); and the subsidiary streets that were formed and thus helped to cover what were once unoccupied spaces came later. As we have seen, Crowther has perpetuated two of the more important residences which formerly stood here—Turret House and Caron House; and he has also left us a picture of yet another—Stockwell Park House.

Miss Priscilla Wakefield, writing her *Perambulations of London* in the year 1809, speaks of Stockwell as a " small rural village," but she was so anxious to get on to Camberwell, " a pleasant retreat for those citizens who have a taste for the country," as she calls it, and where, by the way, Robert Browning was to be born three years later, and, as entomologists will remember, that now very rare species Vanessa Antiopa[1] was first found, that she says nothing further about Stockwell. And truth to tell there are not many, other than residents in the district, who could nowadays probably tell you off-hand exactly where Stockwell is; but if you go along the Kennington Road and press on to its continuation as the Clapham Road, you will find Stockwell Park Road on your left, linking up Clapham Road with Brixton Road; and this may be regarded as the present equivalent to the Stockwell of old days, the " rural village " of Miss Wakefield's observation, and perhaps, if now remembered for anything, chiefly remembered for its " ghost." The name is probably derived from the Saxon *stoc*, a word, and the *well*, from some neighbouring spring of which so many were, in the eighteenth century, discovered in the vicinity.

As the story of the Stockwell Ghost may be unfamiliar to many, I make no apology for " lifting " the account, written by Mackay in his *Extraordinary Popular Delusions*, of that amazing apparition. After

---

[1] It was at Stockwell, too, that Mr. Denyer raised in 1859 a hitherto unknown variety of pear, of which a water-colour is extant, belonging to F. Weston, Esq.

describing the better remembered Cock Lane Ghost of 1762, Mackay proceeds: " About ten years afterwards London was again alarmed by the story of a haunted house. Stockwell, near Vauxhall, the scene of the antics of this new ghost, became almost as celebrated in the annals of superstition as Cock Lane. Mrs. Golding, an elderly lady, who resided alone with her servant, Anne Robinson, was sorely surprised on the evening of Twelfth-Day, 1772, to observe a most extraordinary commotion among her crockery. Cups and saucers rattled down the chimney— pots and pans were whirled down stairs or through the windows, and hams, cheeses, and loaves of bread disported themselves upon the floor as if the devil were in them. This, at least, was the conclusion that Mrs. Golding came to; and being greatly alarmed, she invited some of her neighbours to stay with her and protect her from the evil one. Their presence, however, did not put a stop to the insurrection of china, and every room in the house was in a short time strewed with the fragments. The chairs and table joined, at last, in the tumult, and things looked altogether so serious and inexplicable that the neighbours, dreading that the house itself would next be seized with a fit of motion, and tumble about their ears, left poor Mrs. Golding to bear the brunt of it by herself. The ghost in this case was solemnly remonstrated with, and urged to take its departure; but the demolition continuing as great as before, Mrs. Golding finally made up her mind to quit the house altogether. She took refuge with Anne Robinson in the house of a neighbour; but his glass and crockery being immediately subjected to the same persecution, he was reluctantly compelled to give her notice to quit. The old lady, thus forced back to her own house, endured the disturbance for some days longer, when suspecting that Anne Robinson was the cause of all the mischief, she dismissed her from her service. The extraordinary appearances immediately ceased, and were never afterwards renewed; a fact which is of itself sufficient to point out the real disturber. A long time afterwards Anne Robinson confessed the whole matter to the Reverend Mr. Brayfield. This gentleman confided the story to Mr. Hone, who has published an explanation of the mystery. Anne, it appears, was anxious to have a clear house to carry on an intrigue with her lover, and resorted to this trick to effect her purpose. She placed the china on the shelves in such a manner that it fell on the slightest motion, and attached horse-hairs to other articles so that she could jerk them down from an adjoining room without being perceived by anyone. She was exceedingly dexterous at this sort of work, and would have proved a formidable rival to many a juggler by profession. A full explanation of the whole affair may be found in the *Every Day Book*." [1]

So much for the Stockwell Ghost, which was able, in a credulous generation, to mystify many, but whose antics, like those of so many similar manifestations, were capable of a very simple explanation.

Among the benefactors to Stockwell was a Mr. John Angell, who died in 1784, and left a sum of money for the erection of a home for seven decayed gentlemen, to which were to be attached two clergymen, an organist, six singing men, twelve Christians, a verger, a chapel clerk, and three domestic servants—so that the seven gentlemen were ecclesiastically and musically, as well as materially, well endowed. The sum of six thousand pounds was bequeathed for the building, and £800 a year for the upkeep of this establishment. But, says Allen (*History of Surrey*), who gives these details in 1829, " ever since the death of the testator there has been a suit in chancery respecting his will, and his intentions have, of course, never been carried into effect." [2] Indeed, Angell's will was so curious a one that it might well invoke the law for its proper propounding. The Stockwell property had come into his family through the marriage of his grandfather with Elizabeth, daughter and heiress of John Caldwell of Brixton. John Angell, having made arrangements for his almshouses (their foundation, I may here say, was invalidated by the statute of Mortmain) left the remainder of his property, in default of lineal male issue from his great-great-grandfather, to a Mr. Brown of Studley, in Wiltshire, a relation by female descent, who obtained possession of the legacy and assumed the name of Angell in consequence. The result of the long lawsuit, however, was that John Angell's two sons eventually substantiated their claims, the house and freehold ground being adjudged to the elder, Benedict, and the copyhold portion, of about ten acres, to the younger.

[1] Scott also describes the circumstance in his *Demonology and Witchcraft*.
[2] Angell Park Road perpetuates the name of this would-be benefactor to the district.

I mention this because Mr. Angell lived in a handsome brick house, later occupied as a boarding school, its gardens being ample and well planted with shrubs and trees. This was the Stockwell Park House of which Crowther has left us the two pictures here reproduced.

It stood with its grounds on a site bounded east and west by the Stockwell Park Road and the Stockwell Road, and north and south by Rumsey Road (so called from a property of this name at Calne, in Wiltshire, once belonging to the Angells) and Stockwell Park Walk. The mansion itself occupied approximately the site on which the Baptist Church now stands, and its grounds are cut through by two subsidiary thoroughfares known as Benedict Road and Speenham Road, the former running between the house and the stables, as depicted by Crowther. The triangular piece of railed-in turf in the foreground of the picture is still there, but has been considerably reduced in size. The road shown is the Stockwell Road bearing away to the north-west.

From an earlier view of the mansion (*circa* 1792) we see it abutting immediately on open ground. Then, its façade was thoroughly Georgian with a pediment in the classic style, and nine windows in the first storey. This graceful frontage, with its characteristic doorway, had been, as we see from the accompanying picture, entirely changed, the pediment having been removed, the doorway modernized, and every other window blocked up (in consequence of the window tax, no doubt). The roof alone remains as it was at an earlier time; that and the stable buildings, with their bell-turret. Another change was made by partially pulling down the low wall which had hitherto shielded the front garden from the Common.

The second of Crowther's pictures shows us the garden at the back of the house, where other obvious changes in the structure, from the Georgian convention, will be seen to have taken place. The grounds were not of very great extent, and were bounded by Rumsey Road and the other thoroughfares I have mentioned when describing the house itself.[1]

There was another important house at Stockwell, known as the Manor House, and traditionally, but without adequate grounds, once

[1] I am indebted to F. Weston, Esq., for accurate information as to the exact position of Stockwell Park House, and other data concerning it and its original owners.

STOCKWELL PARK HOUSE, FROM STOCKWELL PARK

STOCKWELL PARK HOUSE

From Stockwell Park

supposed to have been the residence of Thomas Cromwell. The truth is that it was, at that period, the property of Sir John Leigh, who lived there. Lysons, writing in 1792, says the site of this manor house then belonged to a Mr. Barrett, who held the remainder of a thousand years' lease, but Allan, in 1829, speaks of the house as then being inhabited by a butcher. As a matter of fact, the original manor house had been pulled down in 1755, and another one built on its site, probably by the son of the Mr. Isaac Barrett who had obtained his long lease of the ground in 1770, and who, dying in 1808, bequeathed it to his sons, George Rogers Barrett and the Rev. Jonathan Tyers Barrett, a Prebendary of St. Paul's.

At the end of the eighteenth century the village of Stockwell consisted of only one hundred houses! But as a manor it had a very respectable antiquity. It then comprised much of the ground which is now Vauxhall, Stockwell, and South Lambeth, and was known by the last name. In the reign of Henry III it appertained to Baldwin de Insula, who also appears to have owned West Mitcham and South Stretham (Streatham). When Baldwin died the property was valued at £19 16s. 4½d. Later it passed to Margaret de Ripariis, who died here, in 1292. According to Lysons the manor then passed successively to one Thomas Romayne, and after the decease of his widow, to his daughters, among whom it was divided, the portion now represented by Stockwell falling to the share of Rocyse de Boreford. Later, Sir James de Boreford held it, and subsequently it passed into the hands of a certain John Harold, described as a burgess of Calais, who sold it to John Donet and Sir Thomas Swinford, the latter of whom must afterwards have come into entire possession, as he settled it on his wife Catherine, who afterwards became the third wife of John of Gaunt. At a later period the Wynter, Molineux, and Leigh families possessed it in turn, Sir John Leigh dying here in 1524. In 1544 Sir John's son and heir conveyed it to the king.

Having thus become royal property, we find Queen Mary granting the place to Anthony Browne, Viscount Montague, who died, possessing it, in 1592. Whether Mary only granted the property for his life to Lord Montague or whether an exchange for other property was made with his heirs, certain it is that it somehow reverted to the Crown, as it is set down among the manors appertaining to James I. But only two years later it is known to have become the property of Sir George Chute, and was held by his family till it was sold to Sir John Thornycroft, about the end of the seventeenth century. The Thornycrofts continued to hold it, and when Lysons was writing his account of it in 1792 he states that it was then the property of Henry Thornycroft, Esq.

There is an old print of the manor house referred to, showing its front as it was in 1750, with a steep flight of steps leading up to the front door. It was, like Stockwell Park House, on the Common one of those village greens which once were to be found thus close to London, but for which we have now to journey far into the country. Overlooking the green was, too, the Swan Inn, which was at the junction of Stockwell Road and Landor Road. In 1874, not without opposition on the part of the neighbouring inhabitants, the green was cut up and houses built on its site. It is still, however, known as Stockwell Green, although it has lost all claim to the title.

We can reach Battersea through the wilds of Clapham, that maze of streets which run into each other from the Clapham Road, and which the intricacies of railway lines makes worse confounded in their confusion. When we gain Battersea Park we are in a haven of refuge, and for a time can forget the forest of bricks and mortar as represented in this large area, by wandering about the vast pleasance which reflects its greenery in the river, and is full of charming spots of the existence of which so many who live but a stone's throw away across the Thames appear unaware, since those now, as they seem, far-off days when Fashion betook itself to wheels and it was the thing to ride a bicycle in Battersea Park. That area of some two hundred acres was opened in 1858. Its formation was a long and costly business, for the foreshore of the river here had to be embanked, and the land thoroughly drained, with the result that it was found necessary to raise the level of the ground by the addition of a million cubic feet of earth, which, by the bye, was obtained during the excavation of the Victoria Docks, near Blackwall. The amount expended on the work was £313,000. One wonders what such an undertaking would cost to-day at present rates of wages and short hours of work!

STOCKWELL PARK HOUSE

Garaen Front

STOCKWELL PARK HOUSE

Garden Front

STOCKWELL, VAUXHALL, AND BATTERSEA

One of the most attractive features of Battersea Park is the Sub-tropical Garden, covering some four acres, which is said to be the finest thing of the kind open to the public. But to my mind the most charming part of the park is that where it borders the river, and whence the red-brick houses of Cheyne Walk can be seen behind their guardian trees, and the old church stands a sentinel, as it has stood through the ages, rather wondering, one thinks, at the Crosby Hall which has come from the City to bear it company.

It is rather a curious thing that whereas Chelsea is still a name to conjure with, Battersea connotes little beyond its park, and its quaint church, with its steeple rising amid the warehouses and the campanili of commerce. And yet Battersea has a long and interesting history, and if it cannot be said to have been the place of residence of so many illustrious people as have congregated from time to time at Chelsea, it has had, at least, one notable inhabitant in Lord Bolingbroke who, on the lawn attached to his house here, made the famous holocaust of the five hundred copies of *The Patriot King*, the printing of which had been achieved with such an air of mystery. Here, too, such men as Swift, Arbuthnot, Thomson, and Mallet were constant visitors, and Pope is said to have written his *Essay on Man* in a certain room afterwards known as Pope's Parlour. The Bolingbroke mansion was one of vast extent, and is said to have had as many as forty rooms on a floor. It was demolished, or the greatest part of it, in 1778, and a mill of curious construction, originally erected for the grinding of linseed, was set up on its site. By 1808 a brewery had been established here and malt was crushed where linseed had been before. When Sir Richard Phillips took his " walk " in 1816, he found this mill working, and also a portion of the house in which Bolingbroke had been born and where he produced many of his political lucubrations, and whose epitaph (as true as such things generally are) may be read in the neighbouring church.

Another Battersea worthy was that Sir William Batten whose name crops up so frequently in Pepys's *Diary*. In fact, Battersea was at one time and even in the memory of old people, a residential quarter of some importance. One large mansion near the river was York House, the residence of Sir Edward Wynter; another (where my paternal grand-

113

father lived and where my father was born—if I may be forgiven for introducing a personal note) was Hyde House, and I remember we used to have a picture of this Georgian place which seemed, at least to my childish eyes, quite imposing. It was pulled down in my time and houses and streets cover it and its considerable grounds.

But Battersea has not been denuded of all its old houses and picturesque little features. In Vicarage Road may still be seen a charming late seventeenth-century mansion, Devonshire House, with its characteristic cornice and beautiful wrought-iron gateway, cheek by jowl with another house, not so old, but massive, as the later Georgian builders saw to their structures being. Then off the High Street is The Priory, tucked away in its little corner—the Priory which, no doubt, took its name and its pseudo-gothic ornamentations from the taste which Horace Walpole had for a time managed to make prevalent. Here and there, besides, are old bits clinging to life amid so much that is new and so often distressingly banal; and as you look up Vicarage Road to the High Street and catch sight of some of these relics, with their low stature and tiled roofs, you gaze on something that possesses almost a rural air, and might mistake the spot for one in a village street—miles and miles from London's smoke and noise.

If taverns had not such a habit of getting rebuilt they would be the best links with the past we have; for once a tavern (or, as we so much less picturesquely term them, a public-house) always a tavern—or nearly always. Seldom do buildings once allocated to this use depart from the apostolic succession with which they seem to have involved themselves; although exceptions can be found, and curiously enough one of them is close to Battersea Church

The one of which Crowther made a sketch in 1887, the Raven, is, however, not only still there, but, what is surprising, still presents almost the same appearance as it did forty years ago. What it looked like then and looks like now can be seen from the accompanying picture; and it is an interesting fact that the Raven is the only subject which the artist treated that has not either been demolished or very largely altered.

It stands at the corner of Church Road (the thoroughfare in the foreground) and Bridge Road West (that running at right angles to it).

THE RAVEN INN, BATTERSEA

THE RAVEN INN, BATTERSEA

The only changes in the façade are the addition of a string of glazed tiles along the front of the ground floor, and the substitution of plain doors for the recessed one in Church Road and that with an ornamental over-door in Bridge Street West. The Jacobean gables, the ancient timbers of the roof, and its red tiles, are still there as they were in the remote days when this inn was in the centre of Battersea. Its exact age is not known; but although it is first mentioned in the churchwardens' accounts in 1765, it is, of course, far older, and probably dates from the early years of the seventeenth century. References to it as The Black Raven are extant, but it is as The Raven, *tout court*, that it is generally known and called.

Not only is the Raven Tavern itself thus nearly untouched, but the quaint little houses adjoining it in the background remain as they appear in the picture. They form a really delightful collocation of old-world dwellings. In the midst of them will be observed a tree and some railings, and here, lying back from the pathway, is a Georgian house of a more ambitious character, with an entrance in the centre protected by a nice over-doorway of the period.

It is worth while wandering about Battersea looking out for such features, for amid so much that is rather squalid one's search is rewarded, and one appreciates one's finds the more because they are often unexpected.

The last of Crowther's drawings which have been selected for reproduction in this volume is that of old Battersea Bridge, not only for the essential charm and interest of the picture, but because it conveniently brings us back to the spot from which we started on our investigations.

A glance at what the old bridge was like in the 'eighties when this picture was executed will at once show how inadequate it was for modern requirements. That beautiful structure which Whistler has immortalized (indeed he was never tired of recording its features with the gleaming water below and the mists and lights rising on either bank) seemed so obviously doomed for destruction that when it was condemned as unsafe in 1881, two years after the Metropolitan Board of Works had purchased it, few could have been surprised; and the only wonder was that its wooden structure had borne the weight of ever increasing traffic so long.

In early days there used to be a ferry at this spot, and when that was superseded by a bridge this wooden one of nineteen spans was flung across the river. It was erected from the designs of a Mr. Holland in 1771-2, a period when there was a good deal of activity in bridge-building on the Thames. As this part was then a distant portion of the metropolis, if indeed it can be said to have been a part of it at all, a wooden structure was all that was then necessary—and it fulfilled its purpose for just over a century; but when, in 1873, it was taken over by the company formed to erect the Albert Bridge, four of the original spans were converted into two, with raised girders on each side, thus affording wider openings for river traffic. As the bridge in its widest part only measured a little over twenty-three feet, and in certain portions only sixteen feet for vehicular traffic, with a footpath varying from two to four feet, it can well be imagined how inconvenient it was. Luckily it had served as a decorative *motif* for the pencil and graver of Whistler, Way, and others who recognized its artistic charm before it was demolished. In 1881, having been certified as unsafe, it was closed and a temporary footbridge was constructed pending the erection of the present commonplace cast-iron one the width of which is about seven times greater than that of its humble predecessor; and which has nothing to recommend it save its utility. This new structure stands rather to the east of the old one, and it may interest those who like figures to know that it cost £143,000.

It carries the trams across it, and that is something, for it is by these humble means of conveyance that you can best reach this spot from Stockwell; threading in and out of the multitudinous streets which now cover the areas of Clapham and Battersea, where the memory of Lord Macaulay is kept alive by the beautiful old houses, in one of which he lived as a boy in The Pavement of the former, and that of Cowley and Bolingbroke and Pope is hidden beneath layers of development in the latter.

As we pass over Battersea Bridge we are again on hallowed ground, the ground where More lived and Henry VIII visited; the ground which is the Chelsea of imperishable memories. We began our peregrination, as they used to term it when they liked sonorous words, in Chelsea, and with it we take our leave. Nor do I think we could start from, or return

OLD *BATTERSEA BRIDGE, FROM THE* NORTH *BANK*

to, a more entrancing spot, because not only are the essentials of a city there, the red brick matured by age, the smoke and the mist with their alchemy, but somehow we seem to be both in town and country here where the river flows by the greenery of Battersea Park, and the trees of the Embankment mirror themselves in its passing tides. You may sigh often enough for the breeze-blown downs or the flowerful closes of the essential countryside, but after all there are moods (and they are, I think, those that return oftenest and stay longest) when one can say with the poet:

> To me the tumult of the street
> Is no less music, than the sweet
> Surge of the wind among the wheat
>   By dale and down.

INDEX

ABBEY Street, Bermondsey, 92.
Abbot, Archbishop, 105.
Adam, ———, 42, 55.
Adam Street, Strand, 45.
Addison, Joseph, 54.
Adelphi, 45.
Adelphi Theatre 45.
"Admiral, The," 4.
Admiralty, 27, 28, 30, 34, 36.
Admiralty Arch, 31, 33, 34, 44.
Albany, Duke of, 60.
Albemarle, Duke of, 37.
Albert Bridge, 116.
Aldwych, 61.
Almonry, Tothill Street, 38.
Almonry, Whitehall Palace, 36-38.
Alsatia, 73.
Ambry, Tothill Street, 38.
Angel Court, Southwark, 88, 91.
Angel Inn, Strand, 63, 64.
Angell, Benedict, 109.
    John, 109, 110.
Angell Park Road, Stockwell, 109 n.
Anne, Queen, 15, 18.
Anne of Cleves, 2, 9.
Arbuthnot, ———, 113.
Archer, ———, 14.
Army Medical Board, 39.
Arundel, Earl of, 57.
Arundel Hotel, Strand, 54, 58.
Arundel House, Strand, 48 n., 56, 57.
Arundel Street, Strand, 54, 57, 63.
Ashbee, C. R., 3.
Ashby-Sterry, Mr., 78.
Ashmole, Elias, 101-104.

Astell, Mary, 2.
Astley, ———, 65, 101.

Babington, Misses, 10.
Bacon, ———, 89.
Balfour, Jabez, 50.
Bamfield, ———, 52.
Bankside, 101.
Banqueting House, Whitehall, 37, 39, 40.
Barker, Robert, 100.
Barrett, ———, 111.
    George Rogers, 111.
    Isaac, 111.
    Rev. Jonathan Tyers, 111.
Barry, ———, 44.
    Sir Charles, 43.
    Spranger, 50, 54.
Barton Street, Westminster, 24.
Bath and Wells, Bishop of, 57.
Batten, Sir William, 113.
Battersea, 112-116.
Battersea Bridge, 12, 115.
Battersea Church, 113.
Battersea Park, 112, 113, 117.
Baxter, ———, 90.
Beaufoy's Distillery, 102.
Beckwiths, 23.
Bedford Street, Strand, 53.
Bedloe, Captain William, 81.
Bell Inn, Chelsea, 2.
Beloe, Rev. William, 18.
Belvidere Place, Southwark, 90.
Benedict Road, Stockwell, 110.
Bentham, Jeremy, 20 n.
Berkeley, Earl of, 32.

Berkeley, Grantley, 32.
Berkeley House, 32, 33.
Bermondsey, 91-93.
Bermondsey Abbey, 92, 93.
Bermondsey Street, 91-93.
Bethlehem Hospital, 103.
Birch, C. B., 60.
  Dr., 54.
Birdcage Walk, 25.
Black Horse Inn, Westminster, 22.
Black Raven, Battersea, 115.
Blackfriars Road, 94.
Blackheath, 30.
Blackman Street, Southwark, 73, 90.
Blake, Anthony, 79.
Blue Coat School, 17, 18.
Bob Sawyer, 75.
Boehm, Sir Edgar, 1, 60.
Bohemia, Queen of, 65.
Bolingbroke, Lord, 113, 116.
Booksellers' Row, 47, 62.
Booth, Mrs., 4.
  Barton, 24.
Boreford, Sir James de, 111.
  Rocyse de, 111.
Borough, The, 72-91.
Borough High Street, 76, 80, 88, 89, 92.
Borough Road, 89.
Boswell's Court, 61.
Bowling Green, Whitehall, 37.
Bracegirdle, Mrs., 54, 55.
Brandon, Richard, 76.
Bray, Sir Reginald, 7.
Brayfield, Rev., 108.
Brewer's Green, Westminster, 17.
Bridewell Alley, Southwark, 89.
Bridge Road West, 114, 115.
Bridge Street, Westminster, 25.
British Coffee House, 35.
Brixton Road, 107.
Broad Sanctuary, Westminster, 19.
Broadway, Westminster, 17, 20-23.

Brocklesby, Dr. Richard, 54, 58.
Broughton, John, 100.
Brouncker, Lord, 92.
Brown, ———, 95, 109.
Browne, Anthony, 111.
Browning, Robert, 107.
Brummell, 33.
Brunel, Sir Isambard, 27.
Bubb, Captain, 100.
Buckingham, Duke of, 102, 103.
Buckingham Court, Westminster, 30.
Buckingham House and Palace, 3, 44.
Buckle, Henry Thomas, 54.
Bull Head Tavern, 31.
Burdett-Coutts, Baroness, 16.
Burke, Edmund, 58.
Burleigh, Lord, 17.
Burleigh Street, 53.
Burns, John, 12.
Burton Court, Chelsea, 9.
Busby, Dr., 17.
Butcher's Row, 60, 61.
Butler's Almshouses, 16.
Byron, Lord, 25.

Cade, Jack, 76.
Caldwell, Elizabeth, 109.
  John, 109.
Calne, Wiltshire, 110.
Campbell, Thomas, 27.
Canning, George, 31.
Canova, ———, 68.
Canterbury, See of, 98, 99.
Canterbury pilgrims, 66, 71.
Capon, ———, 19.
Capper's Wharf, 51.
Captain Jack, 76.
Carlisle, Bishop of, 99.
Carlisle House, Lambeth, 99.
Carlisle Street, Lambeth, 99.
Carlton House, 34.
Carlyle, Thomas, 7, 9.

INDEX

Caroline, Queen, 30.
Caron, Sir Noel de, 100, 105, 106.
Caron House, 102, 105-107.
Carter, ——, 43.
Cary, Henry, 50.
Castlemaine, Lady, 37.
Castlewood, Lady, 9.
Catherine of Aragon, 9.
Catherine of Braganza, 11 n.
Cavendish, Ada, 65.
Caxton, William, 38.
Caxton Street, Westminster, 18.
Cecil Hotel, 50.
Cecil House, Strand, 50.
Cecil Street, Strand, 50, 51.
Cenotaph, 69.
Chadwyck-Healey, Sir C. E. H., vii.
Chamberlayne, Dr., 6.
Chambers, Sir William, 83.
Chandos House, Westminster, 18.
'Change Alley, 53.
Chantrey, ——, 44.
Chapel Royal, Whitehall, 39.
Chapel Street, Westminster, 18.
Chapman, Richard, 11.
Charing Cross, 29, 30, 34, 70.
Charing Cross Railway Station, 31, 44, 70.
Charing Cross Road, 47.
Charles I, 36, 37, 76, 102, 103, 105.
Charles II, 28, 37, 105.
Charles Street, Westminster, 27.
Charlotte, Princess, 30.
Charlotte Street, Southwark, 94.
Chelsea family, 6.
Chelsea, 1-13, 17, 113, 116.
Chelsea Bridge Road, 12.
Chelsea China Factory, 8.
Chelsea Church, 2, 5-7, 9, 11, 12, 17.
Chelsea Embankment, 8, 9, 11-13.
Chelsea Ferry, 2.
Chelsea Hospital, 9, 12.
Chelsea Hospital for Sick Children, 8.

Chelsea Library, 3.
Chelsea Manor, 7.
Chelsea Manor House, 2, 6, 9.
Chelsea Physic Garden, 6, 12.
Cheltenham Terrace, Chelsea, 9.
Cheney's (Dr.) School, 105, 106.
Cheshire Cheese, Old Square, 56.
Chesterfield, Lord, 14, 30.
Cheyne, Mr., 2.
Cheyne Walk, 1-5, 8, 11, 113.
Christmas, Gerard, 42.
Church Road, Battersea, 114, 115.
Church Street, Chelsea, 8.
Church Street, Lambeth, 101.
Chute, Sir George, 112.
Cibber, Colley, 31.
Civil Engineers, Institution of, 26.
Clapham, 116.
Clapham Road, 107, 112.
Clare, Lord, 25.
Clarence House, 3.
Clarendon, Lord Chancellor, 105, 106.
Clement's Inn, 61.
Clerkenwell, 97.
Clifford Family, 34.
Clink, Southwark, 86.
Clive's Statue, 27.
Cobbett, William, 27.
Cochrane, Lord, 90.
Cock Lane Ghost, 108.
Cockspur Street, 29, 30, 31, 34, 44.
Colet, Humfrey, 79.
College Street, Westminster, 24.
Collett, John, 77.
Colliers' Rents, 89.
Combe, William, 90.
Comptroller-General of Exchequer, 39.
Conduit, Strand, 48.
Congreve, Sir William, 50, 51, 55.
Congreve House, 51.
Costigan, Captain, 64.
Cottington, Sir Francis, 105.

121

County Hall, 71, 72.
Court of Record, 89.
Court of the Marshalsea, 89.
Court of Verge, 89.
Coutts's Bank, 45.
Cowley, ———, 116.
Cowley, Middlesex, 24.
Cowley Street, Westminster, 24.
Cox's Museum, 32.
Craig's Court, Westminster, 30.
Craven, Lord, 65, 81.
Craven House, 65.
Crofts, Lord, 31.
Cromwell, Oliver, 74.
    Thomas, 76, 111.
Cromwell Place, 30.
Cromwell's Palace, 30.
Crosby Hall, Chelsea, 11, 113.
Crosby Road, Bermondsey, 93.
Crowned or Cross Keys Inn, Southwark, 83, 84.
Crowther, J., vii, viii, *et seq.*
Cruden, ———, 2.
Cuper's Gardens, 101, 102.
Cure, Thomas, 82.

Dacre, Lord, 19, 22.
    Gregory, Lord, 17.
    Lady, 6, 17, 18.
Dacre Almshouses, 6, 16-19.
Dacre Street, 17.
Danckerts, ———, 36.
Dane's Inn, 63, 64.
Danvers Street, Chelsea, 2, 3.
Dartford (Darente), Manor of, 98.
David Copperfield, 48, 90, 91.
"Dead Wall," 24.
Dee, Dr., 100.
Defoe, Daniel, 76.
Delahay Street, Westminster, 26, 27.
Delvaux, Laurent, 43.
Denny's Bookshop, 47, 62.

Denyer, ———, 107 *n.*
Derby, 6th Earl of, 6.
Devonshire House, Battersea, 114.
Dibdin, Charles, 2.
Dickens, Charles, 14, 48, 51, 54, 64, 75, 77, 78, 87-91.
District Railway, 23.
Dog Inn, Chelsea, 2, 3.
Dollond, Peter, 100.
Dominicetti, ———, 2.
Don Saltero's Coffee House, 2.
Donet, John, 111.
Doulton, Messrs., 101.
Dover House, 37, 38, 40.
Downing Street, 27, 36.
Drummond's Bank, 30, 31.
Drury Lane, 64.
Ducarel, Dr., 104.
Duck Lane, Westminster, 19.
Dudley, Earl of, 82.
    Lord Guildford, 6.
Duffield, Mary, 82.
Duke Street, Westminster, 26, 27.
Duke Street Chapel, 27.
Dun, Cornelius van, 23.
Dunn, J., 56 *n.*
Dupin, ———, 68.
Dysart, Earls of, 55.
Dysart Hotel, 55.

Edward the Confessor, 98, 99.
Eliot, George, 11.
Eliot-Hodgkin, G., 82.
Elizabeth, Queen, 9.
Elliston, ———, 65.
Embankment Gardens, 51.
Emmanuel Hospital, 17, 18.
"English Hobbema," 100.
Erasmus, 1.
Essex, Earl of, 48.
Evelyn, John, 103.
Exchange Court or Alley, 53.

INDEX

Exeter 'Change, 53.
Exeter House, 53.
Exeter Street, 53.

Ferdinand, 36.
Ferrey, Benjamin, 16.
Fife House, 38.
Fineux, Sir John, 63.
Fisher, Bishop, 99.
Fleet Prison, 106.
Flower, Mr. and Mrs. Wickham, 8 *n.*
Foreign Office, 27.
Forman, Simon, 100.
Formantel, Miss, 12.
Franklin, Mr., 9.
Franklin's Row, Chelsea, 9.
French Church, Spring Gardens, 29.
French Protestant Chapels, 33, 34.

Garrick, David, 7.
Gaskell, Mrs., 11.
Geary, ———, 77.
George III, 25 *n.*
George IV, 33, 34, 44.
George, Sir Ernest, 74 *n.*
George Inn, Southwark, 78-81, 85.
George Inn and Yard, Westminster, 25.
George's Row, Lambeth, 103.
Gibbon, Edward, 24.
Gifford, ———, 81.
Glastonbury, Mr., 36.
Glebe Place, Chelsea, 3.
Globe Theatre, 65.
Goda, Countess, 98.
Godwin, Earl, 99.
Golden Anchor, Strand, 59.
Golden Ball, Strand, 47.
Golden Buildings, 47.
Golden Cross, Strand, 43.
Golden Unicorn, Strand, 47.
Golding, Mrs., 108.
   William, 79.

Goldsmith, Oliver, 7, 25, 76.
Goldsmiths' Company, 39.
Gordon, Lord George, 72, 95.
Gordon Riots, 89.
Great College Street, 24.
Great George Street, 24-26.
Great Hall, The, 40.
Great Northern Railway Offices, 80.
Great Sanctuary, 38.
Great Surrey Street, 94.
Green, Thomas, 79.
   William, 17.
Green Coat School, 17.
Gresham, John, 82.
Grey, Lady Jane, 2.
   of Wilton, Lord, 22.
Grey Coat Hospital, 14-16.
Grey-Coat-Place, 15.
Grey Coat Street, 14.
Griffin, Strand, 60.
Groot, Isaac de, 19.
Grosvenor Place, 43.
Grosvenor Road, Chelsea, 13.
Grotius, Hugo, 19.
Grove, The, 32.
Grover, ———, 81.
Guildford, Lady Jane, 6.
Gun House, 35, 36.
Guy's Hospital, 80, 85.

Half Moon Passage, 66.
Hall, Rev. Newman, 97.
Hamilton, Lord, 2.
   Dr., 34.
Hampden, John, 19.
Hampton Place, Strand, 57.
Hardicanute, 99.
Harold, 98, 99.
Harold, John, 111.
Harvard, John, 84.
Harvard College, 84.
Hastings House, Strand, 55.

Hatherley, Lord Chancellor, 25.
Hawaydyne, ———, 76.
Haydon, Benjamin Robert, 90.
Hazlitt, William, 20 n.
Heathcock Court, 45.
Henry III, 23, 99.
Henry V, 90.
Henry VIII, 2, 7, 9, 17, 99, 116.
Henry Esmond, 9.
Hercules Buildings, 99.
Hereditary Grand Almoner, 38.
Higgins, 27.
High Almoner, 38.
High Street, Battersea, 114.
Hill, Captain, 54.
   Emery, 15, 16.
   Rowland, 94-97.
Hill's Bookshop, 63.
Hogarth, William, 27, 30.
Holbein, Hans, 6, 36, 37.
Holland, ———, 116.
Holland House, 106.
Hollar, ———, 42, 57.
Holywell Street, 46, 47, 61-66.
Hone, William, 90, 108.
Hooker, Sir William, 105.
Hooper, Bishop, 64.
Hopkins, Captain, 91.
Horse Guards Avenue, 37, 41.
Horse Guards Parade, 24, 27, 35-37, 39.
Horse Shoe Alley, 17.
Horseferry Road, 14.
Horsly Downe, 92.
Hospital of Jesus, 17.
Howard Family, 54, 99.
Howard of Effingham, Lord, 2.
Howard Street, Strand, 54-56.
Humbles Family, 82.
Hungerford, Sir Edward, 31.
Hungerford Market, 31, 44.
Hunt, Holman, 8.
   Leigh, 9.

Hunter, John, 7.
Huntingdon, Lady, 95, 97.
Hyde House, Battersea, 114.

Imperial Theatre, Westminster, 23.
Inglis's Warehouse, Strand, 47.
Insula, Baldwin de, 111.
Ireland, Samuel, 54.
Ivy Bridge, Strand, 52.
Ivy, or Ivy Bridge, Lane, 52, 53.

James I, 53, 112.
James II, 14, 26, 28.
James Street, Westminster, 17, 18.
Jansen, Bernard, 42.
Jeffreys, Lord, 26, 27.
Jenkins, Rev. John, 10.
Jenner, Edward, 94.
Jennings, Constantine, 2.
Jerrold, Douglas, 53 n., 64.
John, Augustus, 1.
John of Gaunt, 111.
Johnson, Dr., 7, 19, 58, 66, 85.
Jones, Sir Horace, 60.
   Inigo, 37, 39, 42.
Justice Walk, Chelsea, 8.

Kean, Edmund, 50.
Kennington, 99, 105, 106.
Kennington Oval, 101, 106.
Kennington Road, 107.
Kent, Duke of, 95.
Kent, ———, 27, 36.
King Edward Street, Lambeth, 103.
King Street Gateway, 37.
King Street, Southwark, 91.
King Street, Westminster, 25.
King's Bench Alley, Southwark, 89.
King's Bench Prison, 86, 88-90.
King's College, Strand, 46.
King's Head, Southwark, 80-83.
King's Head Cottages, Westminster, 21.

INDEX

King's Road, Chelsea, 8, 9, 11.
Kingsway, 61.
Kipling Street, Bermondsey, 93.
Knatchbull, Sir Edward, 25.

La Place, 99.
Labelye, Charles, 25.
Lamb, Charles, 20 n.
Lambeth (Lembehith, Lambyth, Lamedh,
    Lamhee, Lamheth, Lanchei, Loamhithe),
    97-112.
Lambeth, South, 111.
Lambeth Church, 104, 105.
Lambeth Marsh, 100.
Lambeth Palace, 99.
Lambeth Proper, 100.
Landor Road, Stockwell, 112.
Landseer, ———, 43.
Lant Street, Borough, 75, 87, 90.
Laud, Archbishop, 102.
Law Courts, 55, 59, 61.
Lawrence Family, 7.
Lawrence Chapel, Chelsea Church, 5, 6.
Lawrence Street, Chelsea, 3, 5, 7, 8.
Layton's Yard, Southwark, 88.
Lee, Jennie, 65.
    Nat, 73.
Leicester, Earl of, 6.
Leigh Family, 111.
    Sir John, 111.
Lemon, Mark, 64.
Lethbridge, ———, 69.
Lever, Ashton, 103.
Lilly, ———, 100.
Lincoln, Earl of, 17.
Lincoln's Inn, 63.
Lindsay House, Chelsea, 2.
Lirriper, Mrs., 54.
Litlington, Abbot, 24.
Little Chapel Street, 17.
Little Dorrit, 85, 86, 88.
Little Shire Lane, 61.

Loamhithe, 98.
Lockitt's, 30.
Lombard Street, Chelsea, 2.
London County Council Offices, 29, 31-33,
    71, 72.
Long Lane, Bermondsey, 92.
Long Lane, Smithfield, 75.
Long Southwark, 79 n., 82.
Lord High Treasurer, 39.
Lords of the Council, 39.
Lyon's Inn, 61, 64-67.

Macaulay, Lord, 25, 116.
Madelaine Bray, 90.
Maiden Lane, Strand, 53.
Mall, The, 3, 35, 44.
Mallet, ———, 113.
Marble Arch, 44.
Market Street, 44.
Marlborough House, 4.
Marshall, Frank, 65.
Marshalsea, 85-89.
Marshalsea Place, 88.
Marshalsea Road, 88.
Martin, Nicholas, 79.
Mary, Queen, 111.
Mary II, 18.
" Mat of the Mint," 73.
Mathews, Charles, 45.
Matz, B. W., 80.
Maunder, Mrs. Elizabeth, 2.
Maunsel, John, 22, 23.
May Pole, Strand, 47.
Mazarin, Duchess of, 9.
Mead Place, Lambeth, 103.
Mechanical Engineers, Institute of, 27.
Mermaid Alley and Inn, 30.
Metropolitan Board of Works, 32, 69, 115.
Meux, Sir Henry, 60.
Micawber, Mr. and Mrs., 90, 91.
Middle Temple, 63.
Milford Lane, Strand, 48, 56.

Military Hospital, Millbank, 13.
Millbank Penitentiary, 13.
Miller, Phillip, 6.
  Thomas, 74.
Milner, Dean, 95.
Milton, John, 20, 31.
Ministry of Health, 25.
Mint, The, 72-74.
Mint Street, 72, 73, 75.
Mitcham, West, 111.
Mitford, Miss, 54.
Mohun, Lord, 54.
Molineux Family, 111.
Monmouth, Duke of, 81.
  Duchess of, 7.
Monmouth House, Chelsea, 7.
Monsey, Messenger, 2.
Montague, Anthony Browne, Viscount, 111.
Montagu House, 37.
Moore, Francis, "Old Moore," 100.
  Tom, 32.
More, Sir Thomas, 1, 6, 17, 63, 116.
Morley's Hotel, 43.
Morris, Sir William, 30.
Mortimer, ———, 54.
Mountfort, William, 54.
Mylne, ———, 42.

Nasmyth, Patrick, 100.
National Bank, 35.
National Gallery, 44.
National Portrait Gallery, 26.
National Schools, 10.
National Society, 10.
Naval and Military Library and Museum, 40.
Needham, Sir Robert, 103.
Nelson Monument, 43, 44.
Neville, Henry, 65.
New Exchange, 53.
New Exchange Alley, 53.
New Inn, 61, 63, 64.

New Pye Street, Westminster, 20.
New Spring Gardens, 31.
New Street, Spring Gardens, 34, 35.
New Tothill Street, Westminster, 20.
Newcastle Court, 61.
Newcomen Street, Southwark, 91.
Newington, 86.
Newington Causeway, 89.
"Niagara," 21.
Nield, ———, 2.
Norfolk, Duke of, 54, 55.
Norfolk Hotel, Strand, 55, 56, 59 n.
Norfolk Row, Lambeth, 99.
Norfolk Street, Strand, 53, 54, 58.
Norman, Dr. Philip, 65, 78, 82, 84.
Northampton, Earl of, 42.
Northumberland, Duke of, 43.
  Duchess of, 2.
  Algernon, Earl of, 42.
Northumberland Avenue, 43.
Northumberland House, 42, 43.

Oakley Street, Chelsea, 9.
O'Connell, Daniel, 25.
Old Pye Street, Westminster, 19, 20.
Old Spring Gardens, 31.
Old Square, Strand, 55.
Oldys, ———, 99.
Olympic Playhouse, 65.
Opéra Comique, 65.
Orchard Street, Westminster, 20.
Orrery, Lord, 27.
Outer Spring Gardens, 30.
Outinian Society, 35.
Oxford, Ashmolean Museum, 101, 102.
Oyster and Supper Rooms, Strand, 45.

Palace Stairs, 37.
Pall Mall, 34.
Pall Mall East, 44.
Palmer, Rev. Edward, 16.
Palsgrave Place, 59.

INDEX

Palsgrave's Head Court, 59.
Pantheon, Clerkenwell, 97.
Pantry, Whitehall, 40.
Paradise Row, Chelsea, 2, 9, 11.
Parliament, Houses of, 19.
Parliament Square, Westminster, 19.
Parr, Catherine, 2.
Parsons, ——, 100.
Pasten, ——, 24.
Paulet, Sir William, 17.
Pavement, The, Clapham, 116.
Peabody Buildings, Westminster, 18, 20.
Peale and Mitchell, 23.
Pear Street, Westminster, 20.
Peel, Sir Robert, 44.
Pembroke, Lord, 36.
Penn, John, 35.
    William, 54, 58.
Pennant, Thomas, 57.
Pepys, Samuel, 22, 92.
Percy Family, 42.
Perker, Mr., 77.
Perkins's Rents, Westminster, 20.
Petty France, Westminster, 20, 21, 23.
Physicians, College of, 44.
Piccadilly, 35.
Pickett Street, 61.
Pickwick, Mr., 77, 78.
Pitt, Moses, 27.
Polish Ambassador, 105.
Polish Association, 27.
Pope, Alexander, 113, 116.
Pope's Head, Southwark, 82.
Porter, Captain, 91.
Poynings, Elizabeth, 83.
    Robert, 83.
    Thomas, 84.
Price, ——, 45.
Prince's Gate, 43.
Prior, Matthew, 27.
Priory, The, Battersea, 114.
Privy Garden, 37.

Privy Stairs, 38.
"Puggy Booth," 4.
Pye, Sir Robert, 19.

Queen Anne's Gate, 24.
Queen Anne's Mansions, 21, 23.
Queen Anne's Square, 24.
Queen's Bench Prison, 85, 88-91.
Queen's Head, Southwark, 81, 83-85.
Queen's House, Chelsea, 2, 11 n., 12.

Rag Fair, 75, 76.
Ranelagh, 12.
Raven Inn, Battersea, 114, 115.
Rennie, John, 68, 74 n.
Richardson, ——, 40.
Richmond Terrace, 37.
Ridler's Bookshop, 62.
Ripariis, Margaret de, 111.
Rising Sun, Chelsea, 3.
Rising Sun, Wych Street, 63, 64.
Robert Allan, 75.
Robinson, Anne, 108.
Rochester, See of, 98.
Rochester Row, Westminster, 15.
Roger de Coverley, Sir, 3, 54.
Roman Bath, Strand, 48, 49.
Romayne, Thomas, 111.
Rose, ——, 99.
Rosemary Lane, 75, 76.
Rossetti, D. G., 1, 2, 4, 11.
Rotunda Chapel, 94.
Royal Army Medical College, 13.
"Royal George," 44.
Royal Mint Street, 75, 76.
Royal United Service Institution, 37-40.
Rummer's Court and Tavern, 30.
Rumsey Road, Stockwell, 110.
Rupert, Prince, 30.
Rushworth, ——, 90.
Ruskin, John, 5, 11.

Rutland, Duchess of, 33.
Rysbrack, ———, 6, 12.

Sackville, Thomas, Earl of Dorset, 17.
　Sir Richard, 17.
St. Anne's Street, Westminster, 19.
St. Bride's Church, Fleet Street, 16.
St. Clement's Danes, 61.
St. Evrémond, Monsieur, 2, 9.
St. George's Church, Borough, 74, 75, 87, 88.
St. George's Circus, 72.
St. George's Fields, 72, 90.
St. James's Park, 20, 26-28.
St. James's Park Station, 21.
St. John the Evangelist, Westminster, 14.
St. John's Wood, 31.
St. Margaret's Church, Southwark, 86.
St. Margaret's Parish, Westminster, 14, 17.
St. Margaret's Hill, 81.
St. Mark's Church, Kennington, 101.
St. Mary le Strand, 46, 48.
St. Mary Overy Priory, 86.
St. Mary's, Whitechapel, 76.
St. Matthew's Episcopal Chapel, 34.
St. Paul's Cathedral, 70.
St. Peter Street, Westminster, 15.
St. Stephen's Church, Westminster, 16.
Salisbury, Lord, 50.
　Robert, Earl of, 102.
Salisbury House, Strand, 50, 52.
Salisbury Stairs, Strand, 52.
Salisbury Street, Strand, 50, 52.
Sam Weller, 77, 78.
Sandys, Lord, 7.
Sans Pareil Theatre, 45.
Sanscroft, Archbishop, 59.
Sargent, J. S., 1, 4.
Scharf, George, 35.
Schofield, Mrs., 79.
Scotland Yard, 39-41, 89.
Scott, Sir George Gilbert, 27, 31.

Scott, John, 45.
　S., 36 n.
　Sir Walter, 45.
　William Bell, 11.
Searle, Mrs., 33.
Serle Street, 61.
Seymour, Lord High Admiral, 2.
　Lord Thomas, 57.
Shakespeare, 75.
Shakespeare's Head, 64.
Shaw, Norman, 41 n.
Sheppard, Jack, 64.
Sheridan, R. B., 25.
Sherman, Rev. James, 97.
Ship Tavern, Westminster, 30.
Shippen, "Downright," 54.
Shordich, John de, 2.
Shot Tower, 49, 70.
Sloane, Sir Hans, 1, 2, 6, 11 n., 12, 103.
"Small Beer Buttery," 38.
Smith, James, 72.
Smith Square, Westminster, 14.
Smithfield, 75, 99.
Smollett, Dr. Tobias, 7, 90.
Snow, Messrs., 59.
　Jeremiah, 59.
Snowfields, 91, 93.
Society of Artists, 32.
Somerset House, 57, 68, 70.
Soult, ———, 35, 36.
South Lambeth Road, 103.
Southampton Street, 55.
Southey, Robert, 95.
Southwark, 71-91.
Southwark Bridge, 74, 81.
Southwark Bridge Road, 74, 88, 90.
Southwark fire, 77, 79, 81, 84.
Southwark Town Hall, 81.
Southwell, Hon. Edward, 33.
Sowerby, ———, 100.
Spa Fields Chapel, 97.
"Spectator," 3.

INDEX

Speenham Road, Stockwell, 110.

Spencer, ———, 77.

Spring Gardens, Westminster, 24, 27-33, 35, 38.

Spring Gardens Mews, 30.

Spring Gardens Terrace, 36.

Spurgeon, ———, 97.

Stafford House, 3.

Stanford, Messrs., 35.

Stanley, Sir Robert, 6.

Stationer, John, 47.

Steele, Sir Richard, 1, 54.

Sterne, Laurence, 7.

Stockwell, 98, 106-112.

Stockwell ghost, 107.

Stockwell Green, 112.

Stockwell Manor House, 110, 111.

Stockwell Park House, 107, 110, 112.

Stockwell Park Road, 107, 110.

Stockwell Park Walk, 110.

Stockwell Road, 110, 121.

Stone Gallery, 37.

Storer, Mrs., 12.

Storey's Gate, 26, 27.

Stourton House, Westminster, 17.

Strahan, Paul & Co., 59.

Strand, 31, 42-67, 99.

Strand Bridge, 47, 52, 69.

Strand Bridge Lane, 47.

Strand Inn, 49.

Strand Lane, 47-49, 52, 56, 57.

Streatham, South, 111.

Street, ———, 55, 60.

Strong, Chevalier, 64.

Strutton Ground, Westminster, 18-20.

Suffolk, Duke of, 73, 75.

　　Earl of, 42.

Sully, Duc de, 57.

Surrey Chapel, 94-97.

Surrey Steps, Strand, 49.

Surrey Street, Strand, 46, 49, 51 n., 55, 56, 58, 59.

Swan Inn, Stockwell, 112.

Swift, Jonathan, 1, 27, 40, 113.

Swinburne, 11.

Swinford, Catherine, 111.

　　Sir Thomas, 111.

Syon House, 43.

Tabard or Talbot Inn, Southwark, 83.

Talbot Inn, Strand, 56.

Tate, Nahum, 73.

Tate Gallery, 13.

Taylor, John, 76, 86.

　　Sir Robert, 31.

Temple Bar, 60.

Temple Bar Tea Rooms, 59.

Tenter Ground, Southwark, 89.

Terry and Yates, 45.

Thackeray, W. M., 24.

Thames, 1, 5, 11-13, 51, 52, 71, 98, 112.

Theobald's Park, 60.

Theodore, King of Corsica, 90.

Thomson, ———, 31, 113.

Thornton, Bonnel, 12.

Thornycroft, Henry, 112.

　　Sir John, 112.

Thorp, John B., 35.

Thorpe, John, 106.

Thurlow, Lord, 25.

Thurtell, ———, 64.

Tivoli Cinema, 45.

Tooley Street, 92.

Tothill Fields, 22, 23.

Tothill Manor, 22.

Tothill Maze, 22.

Tothill, Tuthill, or Tuttle Street, 17, 20, 22, 23.

Tout Court, Southwark, 79.

Tower of London, 89.

Tradescant or Tradeskin, John, 100-105.

Trafalgar Square, 43, 44.

Treasury, The, 36, 37.

Treasury Passage, 36.
"Trial of the Pyx," 39.
Truscott, Sir Francis, 60.
Turner, J. M. W., 1, 4, 5.
Turpin, Dick, 22.
Turret House, Lambeth, 102, 103, 107.
Twining's, 59.
Tyrconnel, Duchess of, 53.

Union Club, 44.
Union Street, Southwark, 94.
United Service Institute. *See* Royal United
    Service Institution.
United Service Museum, 38.
United Westminster Schools, 17.
Upper Cheyne Row, 8, 9.

Vanbrugh, Dame Henrietta, 40.
    Sir John, 40, 41.
Vardy, John, 27.
Vauxhall, 98, 101, 106, 111.
Vauxhall Turnpike, 105.
Vicarage Road, Battersea, 114.
Victoria Docks, 112.
Victoria Embankment, 38, 58.
Victoria Street, Westminster, 19, 20.
Vincent Square, Westminster, 22.
Voltaire, 51 *n.*

Wales, Prince of, 33, 36, 68.
Walker, Frederick, 19.
Wallingford House, 27.
Walpole, Horace, 114.
    Sir Robert, 54.
Waltham, Monks of, 98.
Walton, Izaak, 102.
War Office, 39, 41.
Ward, Rev. John, 81.
Warwick, Sir Philip, 30.
Warwick House and Street, 30.
Watch House, Strand, 47.

Waterloo Bridge, 49, 68-70, 72.
Watson, Sir William, 104.
Watts's Manufactory, 49.
Way, ———, 116.
Weare, Mr., 64.
Webster, Benjamin, 45, 65.
Wellington, Duke of, 69.
Welsh, Mr., 81.
Wesley, John, 72, 95, 96.
Wesleyan Central Hall, 23.
Westminster, 6, 14-67.
Westminster Abbey, 7, 24.
Westminster Aquarium, 23.
Westminster Bridge, 25.
Westminster Bridge Road, 103.
Westminster School, 24.
Weston, J., 107 *n.*, 110 *n.*
Westray, Richard, 83.
Weyland, Mark, 79.
Wheatley, ———, 39.
Whicelo, ———, 92.
Whichcott, Sir Jeremy, 106.
Whistler, J. A. M., 1-4, 11, 115, 116.
White, John, 82.
White Hart, Southwark, 76-79, 82.
White Hart Street, Westminster, 20.
White Horse Inn and Street, Westminster,
    22.
White House, Chelsea, 2.
White Lion Prison, 86-88.
White Lion Tavern, Southwark, 86.
"White Milliner," 53.
Whitehall, 25-27, 30, 35, 37, 89.
Whitehall Court, 41.
Whitehall Palace, 36-40.
Whitehall Stairs, 38.
Whitehall Yard, 39, 40.
Whitelands House and College, 10, 11.
Whitfield, ———, 95, 96.
Wigley's Promenade Rooms, 32.
Wilberforce, William, 95.
Wilkes, John, 7, 25.

INDEX

William III, 27, 40.
Wilson, Albert, 63.
Winchester, Marquis and Marchioness of, 17.
Windsor, St. George's Chapel, 7.
Windymore, Mrs., 18.
Woodfall, ———, 6.
Woolaston, Dr., 50.
Wren, Sir Christopher, 9, 12, 18 *n*., 60.
Wyatt, Thomas, 45.
Wych Street, 61-65.

Wynter Family, 111.
  Sir Edward, 113.

Yates, ———, 45.
York, Duke of, 37, 81.
  James, Duke of, 52.
York House, Battersea, 113.
York Street, Westminster, 17, 20.
Young, William, 41 *n*.

Zazel, 23.